Happy Birthday
Maddie

M000036231

MARINE CORPS B.R.A.T.
Threatening the Status Quo
By Kylee N. Robinson

Kylee N. Robinson

Copyright © 2020 Kylee N. Robinson

All rights reserved.

ISBN: 978-1-7352609-0-7

CO MPASS
Living

Compasslivingri.com

*Neither the United States Marine Corps nor any other component of the Department of Defense has approved, endorsed, or authorized this product (or promotion, or service, or activity)

This book is dedicated to:

My Dad, for being the Marine that made me a B.R.A.T. and the Father that would never let me give up.

My Mom, for going above and beyond every single day without ever truly being recognized and appreciated for what moms do day-in-and-day-out.

My husband, who said "Are you ever going to write that book?" The challenging statement I needed to finally just do it.

And to Kathy Nickel. She is the reason approximately 27,382 contractions were removed and if you don't cry and still like me by the end of this, thank Kathy.
(Left that contraction there just for you *wink wink*)

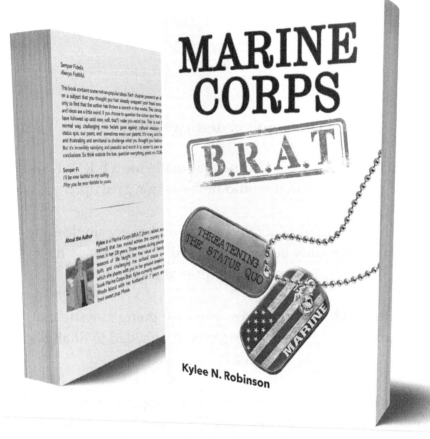

Download the Audiobook FREE!

Read This First:

Marine Corps B.R.A.T. audiobook will be available
September 1st 2020. Get yours 100% FREE by visiting
compasslivingri.com & entering your email address.

Contents

__Foreward__

By Tim Horner

In my 42 year career as a business owner and President and CEO I have constantly challenged myself to adapt and grow. I have always been an observer of my associates and employees. I look beyond their work responsibilities and try to see the whole person. In our company, we believe and understand that all people have worth given to them by God. All have gifts and talents specifically for them. And the more I got to know Kylee Robinson, the more I saw a gifted young lady.

For all of these years I have always been the "boss." Always making decisions for my associates and the business. During this time I have also been a voracious reader (so is Kylee). I value the experiences of others.

Kylee Robinson has been an independent contractor for our company, Premier Designs, for over ten years. As she started to climb the leadership ranks to some of our top levels I watched her closely. I realized that she was mature beyond her years and I wanted to know more about her. I listened closely as she trained thousands of our people from a live stage. As I watched her I saw that she not only "talks the talk" but she also "walks the walk." The more I got to know her the more I saw this young lady's integrity and credibility. That goes a long way with me. So when Kylee sent her *Marine Corps B.R.A.T* manuscript to my wife, Peggy, and me asking if we would read it we said yes immediately.

So it is with that attitude I opened Kylee's manuscript. I wanted to read what this young author had to say. And I can sincerely state that I have never read a book quite like hers.

Marine Corps B.R.A.T. hooked me from the start. As she explains in her book, she wasn't raised to be "normal." Her writing is personal and authentic. Almost autobiographical at times. You will get to know her very well through these chapters and pages. I also got the sense that Kylee is something of a rebel. But in a very positive use of that word. Her parents taught her to question literally anything and everything. No subjects were off limits in her family.

As a result, I was challenged to think differently about serious topics such as education, work, values and faith. And the more I read I found that my life priorities became more of a personal target. With a large and growing family and multiple businesses and associates my priorities can often become skewed. She rationally reminds the reader of the value of time that can be misused with misplaced priorities.

To be completely honest, I wasn't expecting to learn anything much from this young author. At my age, you would think that I would be beyond her experience. But again, I was mistaken. I found myself agreeing with her over and over. I felt connected. Something she values and spends time on in her chapter titled "Community."

Kylee's writing style allowed me to feel as if I were listening to her talk. I could sense her passion and confidence in her topics. It was almost as if we were having a conversation but she was doing both the "asking" and the "answering." This is why I stayed hooked to the end. I tend to have a "please get to the bottom line" mindset. I don't want to be left hanging for long. Kylee always got there at just the right moment. She never lost me as a reader. Another personal measurement of a book for me is when I catch myself saying "Yes! That's it!" frequently.

To me, *Marine Corps B.R.A.T.* is in some ways an autobiography of Kylee's maturing. She shares about growing up and what she was taught by her parents. They shaped her and her siblings as they were homeschooled. They taught all of their children to be independent and to ask questions as a requisite to learning. You will sense that her parents were the strongest influence and inspiration for her. The confidence that comes from a loving and disciplined home is very evident. Her transparent, independent and honest writing style is so refreshing. She is her own person. She states candidly that persons "...in our culture today could use a gallon more independence in them." She would prefer that all of us claim responsibility for our own lives.

As I have been sharing, these chapters are full of personal challenges. But I must not be remiss in sharing my most important "That's it!" topic. Kylee gives a roadmap for many of life's most significant priorities. But deeply undergirding all of those are the Biblical principles that she believes lead to true success in life. I was moved when she so honestly mixed

Biblical truth with today and eternity. She aptly quotes C.S. Lewis, "Human history is the long terrible story of man trying to find something other than God which will make him happy."

In my life and career there have been times when my convictions were challenged and I had nothing but my personal faith to see me through. Kylee shares very openly and personally what her faith means to her. She hones in on the meaning of her relentless pursuit of a servant life. She has a deep faith that leads her to a life of serving others. That is the truly successful life. She asks you to find your faith and be sure of your eternity. An eternity that only Jesus Christ can give you.

So, if you are at all like me you will find this book both instructional and inspirational. At times it is direct, honest and "in your face."

Kylee's words will challenge you to challenge yourself. And please, do not assume you have heard all of this before! So turn the page and get started.

Tim A. Horner

Tim Horner
President
Premier Designs, Inc
DVTD®

1. The Chapter Before the Chapters

"First to fight for right and freedom
And to keep our honor clean
We are proud to claim the title
Of United States Marine"
      - Excerpt from the *Marine Corps Hymn*

"The number one reason people fail in life is because they listen to their friends, family and neighbors."
      - Napoleon Hill

At the end of each year my husband and I sit down for our annual "goal date." The date I look forward to all year. We conduct a mini version of this each month, but this is the big kahuna. The one where we make a whole evening of it. We intentionally take time to dream together, share our ideas and plan, not only for the year ahead, but look at the next five and 10 years based on what we achieved in the past year. A bottle of wine, Christmas tree lights, an evergreen candle and of course *two* whiteboards, dry-erase markers, notebooks, pens and we have the makings of our annual date. We started this tradition early in our marriage and it is one of my favorites.

At the end of 2018, as we were knee-deep in dreaming and scheming, Josh said to me, "Do you still want to write a book? Then when are you going to do it?" Naturally I said, "This year." Not necessarily because I wanted to, but because his questions felt like a challenge. He likely did not mean it as a challenge but it does not take much for me to feel like someone is challenging me. Unsure of where to begin, I sought out some guidance on how to get started. For my whole life I have been writing not knowing where it would lead. There are dozens of documents on my computer of ideas, thoughts and half completed potential chapters. However, I had no realistic, fully fledged out idea for an entire book. That felt daunting. Immediately I felt unqualified. Though, at the same time I thought, "There are way too many *incompetent* people who have written books, *surely I* can manage it!" Therefore, I found some guidelines, came up with my idea, my chapter topics and here we are. Although I made great progress early and had high hopes of finishing the writing process by the end of the summer, I am proud to say that it was completed by the end of the year.

That is how I finally decided to sit down and write. Because, well goodness, if other people can do this so can I! Also, I better knock out the first one before we start our family, because Lord knows I will never have this kind of free time again in my life. May as well figure out what this process looks like so I am ready to go when the time comes to write the next one!

Why Marine Corps B.R.A.T.? If I do not even embody the true nature of this title, why be so bold to title my book with it? Because of everything *it* and I stand for. The three primary Marine Corps values are: honor, courage, commitment.

Marine Corps B.R.A.T.

Even though my dad left the Marine Corps when I was five, these values did not leave our home. These values are the bedrock of the character of each Marine and I like to think they make up the character of each individual in my family as well (or at least we are all trying to live up to them). They are the foundation of the Corps and of our home. These three values, handed down from generation to generation, have made the U.S. Marines the Warrior Elite - which I am pretty sure is what my parents tried to make us too.

Do not hear me wrong, my dad was no Great Santini (thank God!). There was no 5am bugle call or sunrise runs through the woods in camo pants. I am sure that is what you are envisioning. Obviously, Marine and homeschooled equals drill sergeant dad and classroom time learning military acronyms and strategy. Wrong. What it *did* mean is that our home, our schooling and the parenting we received was centered around these things. That integrity and honor are important. It takes courage to take life head on and do big things that matter and commitment to be a successful, useful and loving human being. You can boil our childhood and training down to these things. This is what we were taught to live by. Quitting was never an option in our home. We were taught to work hard, to challenge ourselves and to always stand up for what is right, not what is popular.

That is what this book is about. It is about those values which were engrained into me and why they are important. It is about going against the grain. Because the grain says not to mess with the status quo. "Normal" in our society says that you attend public school, follow that up with college and graduate with an average of $35,000 (per person) in student loans. "Normal" says to live with your significant other and wait to get married until you are nearing 30 and then you are very likely going to get divorced in about eight years. "Normal" is questioning whether right or wrong exists. "Normal" is claiming tolerance of everyone's opinions and viewpoints but throwing a fit when someone disagrees with you or claims a religious freedom that you do not personally observe. "Normal" is blaming the world when you are not where or who you want to be when you want to be it. "Normal" is keeping up with the Joneses, impressing other people, lacking your own opinions and thinking the way you are told to think.

Well…I was not raised to be normal. We challenged "the system" at every turn and nothing has changed since becoming adults.

Homeschooled, military, moving, married at 20 years old and the challenging continues. While my husband graduated with his bachelor's degree, I opted to finish my associates degree and call it a day. We rented and lived well below our means, saying "No" to everything in order to pay off our remaining $44,000 of student loans in 26 months. We have been married for almost eight years and now, as we begin our family, we are choosing to adopt internationally first. We live in New England, we own guns and you are right to assume that all I need to say about my political views is "I'm from Texas."

Marine Corps B.R.A.T.

We are weird, are out of place, very out of our element and loving it. We go against the grain, we buck the system and I have never lived by the status quo. That is why this chapter is first, to let you know what you are getting yourself into. If we met in person I would be very polite and ask lots of questions about you. Unless we spent more time together and you asked me a lot of questions, you would never know about the strong opinions you will find in this book. Not because I am hiding who I am and what I think but mostly because many of these opinions do not make fast friends.

There is a frame of mind currently prevalent that goes something like this: "People suck." For a season I bought into this. People can be aggravating. Similar to how Mrs. Banks in Disney's *Mary Poppins* refers to men, "Though we adore men individually, we agree that as a group they're rather stupid." We can occasionally feel this way about the human race. However, I recently realized this thought process is wrong. The Bible says that people are the most important thing in the whole world. Jesus Christ pulled Himself away from heaven and all its glory for *people*. During His time on earth He constantly allowed Himself to be interrupted from what He was doing for the sake of people. People were everything to Him and if I am to live like Him then people ought to be my priority. At times we can be a pretty terrible race. However, my mission is people. Caring for them, befriending them and liberating them. We have each been given a special skill set that is meant to care for people and I am determined to use my powers for good. If we meet in person I will use those skills to befriend you, care for you and get to know you. However, writing a book is different from a one-on-one conversation. This is where it is (relatively) safe to share my views and opinions, in a different manner, this is using my skill set to serve people.

Do not get me wrong, this is terrifying. I asked my sweet husband to read the first chapter I wrote. As he read, I paced around the house sure that every word I had typed was garbage and he would hate it all. His opinion of that first chapter was the furthest thing from that and I am learning that these feelings come along with the writing process. It is putting all of you out there. It is allowing others into my own inner sanctum, exposed to opinion and criticism. It is the most vulnerable thing I have ever done and, generally, I am terrible at vulnerability. However, it is necessary, it is growth and it is for you. And it is also for me. In the research I have done for this project I have read over and over again to "Write for yourself." Which is baloney because if I were writing for myself I would put it in my journal where no-body else will ever see it. At the same time the experts tell you to write for yourself, they ask you who your audience is. Obviously my audience is myself because that is what they just told me to do! What it means is that you have to write something you would want to read, something you think is of value. You have to be proud of what you have written in order to numb yourself from the potential negative opinions and criticisms that are bound to come your way. Have an audience, yes, but be proud of what you have done before it has ever made a dollar, gotten a rating or been issued a re-view. Be more vulnerable than you have ever been in your lifetime and then toughen your skin and take pride in your work and just accept that some people are going to hate it.

Marine Corps B.R.A.T.

Soon after moving to Rhode Island I joined a women's volleyball league in an effort to stay in the game and meet new friends. It was nerve wracking. Turns out everyone was around 30+ and I was a "baby" among them at 22. Mostly, I kept my mouth shut in an effort to not sound dumb, and picked at the sides of my thumbnails until they bled. A habit I picked up in middle school when I found myself in particularly nerve wracking situations. It is the only real telltale sign that I am feeling anxious because I will rarely admit it. Feeling pretty okay about myself one day in the pregame huddle chit chat and one of the girls makes the comment, "I didn't really begin to not care what people thought about me until I was 30." "*Thirty*?!" I thought. "I have to wait until I am 30 to get over this feeling and bleeding thumbs?!" Well, here I am at 28 with 30 just around the bend and while I have not achieved the desired "I-don't-care-what-you-think-about-me" enlightened state, I have certainly improved and am moving towards it. This book is a labor of love in that direction.

The topics in this book have been discussed with many people over the years and it amazes me how much about this stuff people do not know. How so many have never had some of these thoughts before or ever challenged the path someone else set them on. It saddens me and I long for them to have freedom in their thoughts, freedom to think differently from the way they were told to think.

This may seem like a hodgepodge of topics and as much as this project has been my baby for the past year and a half, I hear that, as a writer you look back and laugh at your first work. So, I promise to you, I will get better from here. Being a writer means putting yourself out there and it is the scariest thing I think I have ever done. Ask me to pack a home and move to a new, strange state and I will have it done in half a second. However, ask me to be vulnerable, sharing all my strongest opinions and thoughts with the world and I think I would much rather die. But here I am. And here you are.

I hope this book brings you freedom, above all else that you discover some sort of freedom in these pages.

2. Attitude & Thoughts

"To change your circumstances, first start thinking different-ly. Do not passively accept unsatisfactory circumstances, but form a picture in your mind of circumstances as they should be. Hold that picture, develop it firmly in all details, believe in it, pray about it, work at it, and you can actualize it according to that mental image emphasized in your positive thinking."
- *The Power of Positive Thinking*
by Norman Vincent Peale

"What we BELIEVE in the subconscious we usually get. Unless <u>faith</u> controls the subconscious, you will never get any good thing, for the subconscious gives back only what your real thought is."
- *The Power of Positive Thinking*
by Norman Vincent Peale

"A man is what he thinks about all day long."
- Ralph Waldo Emerson

"No one can MAKE you feel anything" my dad said sternly as I sat on the floor of our home office. A mere 15 year old dealing with a bullying situation that I will carry with me as a lesson and scar for my entire life. It was yet another day returning home from volleyball practice in tears. High school volleyball is not supposed to be that emotional or intense. As I lamented the afternoon's bullying woes to my parents my dad embraced this teaching moment. The young teenager in me did not feel like it helped and was a little miffed about his lack of understanding to my hurt and venting session. The "Type-A" in me appreciated the guidance he was offering towards fixing the problem but was also annoyed that the solution did not involve changing *them*. "No one can *make* you feel anything" he repeated. "Only *you* have control over how you feel. Do not give someone else that kind of power over you." There were probably some additional sage words of advice but this is the part I remember. The part that, like the whole bullying ordeal, will stay with me for my entire life.

Obviously, I argued with him, because I was a teenager. However, look at that statement again. What is there to argue about? Clearly, I lost. Going to bed I did not feel helped, that the problem was resolved or even relieved from a solid vent. Although I did go to bed thoughtful. I am in control of my feelings. Teenage girl with whacked out hormones coming at you. Maybe that is what my dad was trying to get at, not the issue at hand, rather thinking, "Oh dear God here is an opportunity to speak something into this hormonal mess I am dealing with day in and day out!!" Whatever his motive, whether sage fatherly advice, or "Good grief take a chill pill child" the words stuck with me.

Did I show up at volleyball the next day, feeling confident, less judged, and less inferior? Probably not. But the words kept ringing in my head. Do I presently show up everyday feeling confident, less judged and less inferior? Definitely not. However, it takes practice and repetition for a lesson to stick. Apparently I am still learning and practicing.

Maybe you feel like I did that day, sitting on the floor, vulnerable, beaten down, frustrated and discouraged because of something that was said or done to you. You have all these feelings (it is not only 15 year old girls who have *all* the feelings) and it sure *feels* like what they did or said *made* you feel that way. They *made* you feel judged, feel inferior, feel less than, feel discouraged or feel like a wuss. These are all frustrating feelings. It can be even more frustrating to be reminded that you are the only one who has the power to *make* you feel any way. That statement, which was intended to be helpful, can feel like a smack in the face because when you are feeling down it inadvertently says that you are the one who put yourself there. Rather, your human-ness put you there. It is your job, within your control, to pull yourself out of it. To decide how long you are going to be in that place. The power is yours. Other people can say or do things that jostle us, but ultimately, it is up to us to choose our feelings.

The problem is that feelings are strong and real. The things that cause those feelings are often equally strong and real. This is not suggesting that the guy who flipped you off in traffic *made* you feel so angry you *had* to go home and have a cocktail. Those kind of feelings we can usually handle. It is when real life and real relationships knock us upside the head that the feelings get real. The feelings *appear* to be reality. They seep into our thoughts and attitudes. We begin to believe the feelings because they are strong. They have clouded our rational thinking and we believe that we *are* the feelings. That this is truth and the way life is. I *am* a loser. I *am* inferior. I *am* judged everywhere I go. Nobody likes me. I *am* the problem. It is my fault he flipped me off. I will never be good enough. I will never have close friends again. Etc. [Insert your own strong feeling and belief attached to it here].

It does not have to be this way. My dad said, "No one can *make* you feel anything." You have complete control over your feelings. It may not feel that way but that is the real truth. That is reality. Your current feelings are not reality.

This is not a normal way to handle things. Present culture gives us myriad other methods to handle big, strong feelings: venting, gossiping, alcohol, drugs, comfort food, "a good cry" movie, retail therapy, you name it. The only movie I have ever seen to loosely recommend "taking every thought captive" was Disney's *Doctor Strange*. That movie is not exactly conveying the idea that mere earthly civilians should (or could) do the same as a Marvel Avenger.

Think differently about doing things another way than our pop culture recommends you do them. You are in control of your mind, what you think and what you feel. It is up to you to take every thought captive in order to decide what should be done with it.

- You think 60,000-90,000 thoughts per day.
- 95% of those thoughts are the same as the ones from yesterday.

- If you entertained thoughts of inferiority, anxiety, discouragement, or negativity yesterday - you will be thinking those today too.
- Your mind processes 50 bits per second.
- Your unconscious mind *always* agrees with your conscious mind.
- Unconscious mind processes 11 million bits of data per second.[1]

We have to address thoughts before they are stored in the subconscious mind otherwise, once installed, they are much harder to reverse.

Step One: Decide to change your thinking

Simply because you pick up a book to help you change your thinking does not mean you really want to change your thinking. Saying you want to change something, does not make it true and does not cause the change immediately. Unfortunately, making decisions and changes takes more than a brief statement. It requires deep insight, decision and intense action. Decide for yourself, do you really, truly, deep down in the depths of who you are, desire to think differently than you do right now? Is this change important to you and why?

---

[1] https://tlexinstitute.com/how-to-effortlessly-have-more-positive-thoughts/
National Science Foundation 2005 study
https://www.britannica.com/science/information-theory/Physiology

If you keep thinking the way you have been thinking your actions *will* follow suit.

"Watch your thoughts for they become words
Watch your words for they become actions
Watch your actions for they become habits
Watch your habits for they become character
Watch your character for it becomes your destiny."
   - Lao Tzu

Luke 6:45 (ESV)
"The good person out of the good treasure of his heart produces good, and the evil person out of his evil treasure produces evil, for out of the abundance of the heart his mouth speaks."

1 Minute Application: What is one overarching theme that consistently plays in your mind's thoughts that you would like to change? (Example: the theme or message that you are not good enough, or that you do not have what it takes, or that you cannot do it, etc...)

Step Two: Pay attention to your thoughts

2 Corinthians 10:5 (ESV)
"We destroy arguments and every lofty opinion raised against the knowledge of God, and take every thought captive to obey Christ."

Consider each thought. Well that sounds outrageous. How can I have up to 90,000 thoughts in a day and take every one of them captive? You are already doubting young padawan.

A) Remove distractions

Distractions come in a variety of shapes, sizes, colors, names, faces, etc. The distractions in your life might be work or deadlines. They could be Netflix binging, keeping a schedule or keeping up with the Joneses. Or it might be the ultimate distraction, social media and your phone. You must determine what is in your life that classifies as a distraction. What is taking your mind to places it should not go?

About six months into my married life we invited some friends over for dinner. This particular couple, whom we had known since childhood, had just gotten engaged. As they left our home that night and we reviewed the evening's conversations I finally said, "Why do we hang out with them? Every time they leave we gossip about them." It was only between me and my husband. However, we proceeded to balk about their life choices, things they said, ideals they had (that were clearly "wrong"), and all the ways we disagreed with them that made us "better" than them. Despite feeling superior to them we still always left the get-together unhappy. We did not necessarily enjoy our time with them, it just seemed like the thing to do. We had begun to rekindle the relationship and it seemed like we should continue moving forward. Suddenly, I realized that doing so was not a requirement. If this relationship left us with thoughts of unwholesome superiority and a constant gossip of what had just happened, then why were we pursuing it? That is not who either of us wanted to be so why foster a relationship that caused that?

Had we seen a reason to maintain this relationship for the good of those people, it would have been an entirely different matter. If you feel a moral obligation to an individual, stick with that until you feel God has released you from that situation. In this case, we were doing this purely of our own will. So we stopped. We stopped inviting them over. In making this decision, we noticed they never invited us to do anything. Therefore, the relationship ended. We learned that we are in control of who we spend our time with. If we do not like them, if they do not build us up, if they cause us to do, say or think things that we do not want to, we can prevent that. We can choose to not hang out with those kinds of people. Those kinds of people are a distraction. We eliminated that distraction from our lives.

Obviously, we cannot cut out every distraction. My phone is within reach most of the time. You may have a coworker who is a festering negative Nancy. Or you may really enjoy a good Netflix show. That is okay. What is not okay, is continuing to subject yourself to things that do not build you up or that are not edifying. Take quick stock of your life: what are you doing, watching, participating in or hanging around, that does not align with who you want to be? Perhaps some distance from your phone or a change of Netflix shows might be in order. We can not eliminate all the distractions, but we can limit some, adjust some, and every now and then simply take stock of what we are surrounded by and filling our minds with.

1 Minute Application: What is one distraction in your life right now that you would like to eliminate or lessen?

B) Carve out time each day for silence

The busyness of life can keep us entertained, distracted and stimulated 24/7 if we let it. However, *you* have control. It may seem like you do not have control when you are a busy mom of small children or you hold a demanding, all hours type of job. However, I guarantee you can find some silence in your day if you prioritize it. Decide when and how long that time will be and stick with it. This time allows you a moment to pause, reflect and review your thoughts. What are you thinking? Are these thoughts from yesterday? Are these the kind of thoughts I want to entertain today? Do I need to discard or replace any of these thoughts? Is this thought positive or negative?
Whether it is while driving, in the shower, or while doing housework, carve out a specific pinch of time to think over what is occupying your mind. Your thoughts paint a picture of who you are.

1 Minute Application: Schedule five minutes of quiet into today right now. Maybe put down this book now and set a timer to reflect on this. Find the time.

C) Filter your thoughts through the truth of God's Word

A filter is defined as a pass through device to remove un-wanted material.

We had a pool for most of my childhood. For me, I think of a filter as the white basket we had to clean out of the pool everyday. The basket filtered in unwanted materials that made their way into our sparkling water and it was our job to empty the basket. If the basket got too full of junk it would begin to spit stuff back into the pool. It was a daily task to clean it out.

Thoughts of all kinds are going to make their way into your brain in a given day. It is your job to pause, reflect and filter all those bad thoughts into one place. If you do not do this daily and clean it out, the negative thoughts will begin to spill out into your life. You need a moment of quiet each day and a guide to show you how to filter.

Use Philippians 4:8 (ESV) to serve as a guide to filter your thoughts:
"Finally brothers, whatever is true, whatever is honorable, whatever is just, whatever is pure, whatever is lovely, what-ever is commendable, if there is any excellence, if there is anything worthy of praise, think about these things."

Hold each thought and determine if it matches one of these words.
- True
- Honorable

- Just
- Pure
- Lovely
- Commendable
- Excellent
- Worthy of praise

Do I want to dwell on this thought? What kind of person will this thought make me?

<u>1 Minute Application</u>: Write down Philippians 4:8 (yes, do it old school with a pen and paper), put it somewhere you can see it. And/or list these attributes out on paper.

D) Reject wrong thinking and replace it with truth

Have you ever tried to take something from a toddler? Not the best idea. Toddlers are ticking time bombs. If they are content, healthy, not in danger or hurting anyone, for goodness sake, leave them alone! However, if they have scissors you may need to step in. Taking the item is not the problem, it is the aftermath of the action. The key to managing the "take something from a toddler skill" is to replace the item. You have just left their hands empty and they may feel tricked, confused, or frustrated. Their hands are empty so they know something is wrong. Something just happened against their will. Replace the item. Do not give the toddler the scissors back, find something else entertaining or pleasing to the child that can replace the item you removed. They are feeling a void due to the removal and you need to fill the void or suffer the consequences.

When you remove negative thoughts from your mind you must fill the void. You have left an empty space that begs to be refilled. You might not experience a time bomb toddler in your mind, but if you leave the space empty the negative thought will creep back to its former home. Remove the negative thought, but do not leave the space empty else your efforts are rendered useless. You may have removed the danger for a moment, but peace will not last.

Demolish the old (bad) thoughts in order to make room for new thoughts. New, fresh thoughts and beliefs must fill the empty space. Thoughts that are positive and true. The Bible offers a tremendous amount of truth that you can utilize for this purpose. Something as simple as, "I am worthy. I am smart. I am beautiful. I am a badass," will also suffice if you work hard to believe that statement. We can say these types of statements and not believe them in our core. Remember, the subconscious mind is tricky and stuck in its ways. If you have believed something negative about who you are for a long time, it is going to take some time, and a lot of repetition, to replace those beliefs. Words (whether your own or someone else's) become thoughts, thoughts become beliefs, and beliefs make up your actions, your character, and ultimately, who you are. Are the words you are saying to yourself leading to the character you want to possess?

1 Minute Application: What is one positive thought that you truly believe about yourself?

20

E) "This" rather than "*not* this"

Studies have shown that positive reinforcement in the work-place leads to higher production and morale. This means that when a manager is encouraging, cares about their team as individuals, offers financial rewards for a job well done, etc., the team will perform better, enjoy their working environment and care more about their job. This boost of morale leads to less turnover, a better working atmosphere and more business.

On the other hand, managers who do not know their team's names, barks orders, or never acknowledges a job well done either by words or financial reward will experience a higher turnover environment in their business or department. Positive reinforcement spurs people forward in every situation. When someone says you have done a great job, you feel good and want to do more. When people show pride in us or our work it feels good. When someone says "You suck" you do not want to do a better job for them. Even something such as, "I can see you worked really hard on this and it looks great for a start, maybe we can tweak a couple things," prevents a person from feeling discouraged because they received encouragement as well as guidance rather than a failing grade and a harsh word.

The same thing happens in our minds with our thoughts. Changing a habit is difficult, and often we beat ourselves up for struggling with the process. We may catch ourselves thinking something negative and respond to ourselves with something like, "Stop thinking that! Gosh, will you ever get this right? Don't think that, don't think that, don't think that." This is negative reinforcement. It causes you to feel beaten down, discouraged and like a failure, all of which are thoughts and feelings that we are trying to demolish. Yet, we are reimplementing them as we try to reject them. It can be a vicious cycle.

Instead of "Don't think *this*" we must think "Think *this*." Instead of, "Stop thinking that you are not good enough" we must change that thought and replace it with "I am good enough."

For just a moment I want you to not think about a purple giraffe.

During this writing my husband and I were in the process of house hunting for the first time. We placed two offers in two months and were outbid on both. House hunting is not my favorite thing. When you place an offer on a house you have no idea how quickly a seller is going to get back to you. Naturally, there is a chain of communication their answer must go through before it reaches us. It is incredible to me how draining this waiting can be. It pulls on you emotionally and mentally and therefore affects you physically. All you want to do is get back to "normal" and focus on other things. Telling myself "Don't think about it" does not work. If I am really going to get away from thoughts of that house and our pending offer I must fill my mind with something else. Completely submerge myself in a task, thought, conversation or relationship that leaves no room for me to focus on the house. In fact, writing this helped distract me from the fact that the housing market (at the time) was weird in our state and from my irritation that we had not found something yet. This process gave me another thing to focus on when my mind wandered towards discontentment. We want to remove distractions, however, recognize that the purpose of removing distractions was for identification of our thoughts. To give yourself space to review what thoughts are crossing through your mind.

Are you still picturing a purple giraffe when I told you not to?

As my last story displayed, telling you to *not* think of a purple giraffe did not remove the thought from your mind. In fact, you had probably never pictured a purple giraffe in your life until you read that. Then into your mind popped a purple giraffe.

Saying "Don't think that" will not work. Replace the thought with something you *do* want to think.

1 Minute Application: What is one positive and true thought/phrase/sentence you can use to combat the overarching negative theme you identified in your mind in the Step One application?
(Example: "I am not good enough" combatted with "I am good enough". Or "I can't do this" combatted with "I can do all things through Christ who strengthens me" etc...)

F) Repetition for success

Likely, you have had to practice something in your life. Perhaps it was a sport, a script, an instrument, a monologue, a motion or a specific movement. Learning to walk and run was technically something that we all needed to practice. Practice is repetitive. It is the only time doing the same thing over and over again and expecting a better result is not considered insanity. My parents put me in soccer when I was four years old. One day they told me to go get ready for practice and without hesitation I told them I was not going today. When they asked why, I very determinedly told them, "Because I already went to practice before and I know how to do it now." These are tell tale signs that you have a black and white, type-A child. Do not miss the signs! Things take practice in order to be good at anything. Most people are not child prodigies. Babe Ruth was the home run king only because he was also the strikeout king. The old adage, "Practice makes perfect" is not only a phrase, it is truth. It takes 10,000 hours of doing something to be considered a professional. Practice is repetition. Do not think for a second that you have made the decision to change the way you think and it is just going to happen. It takes practice. It takes repetition.

My mom used the famous mom phrase "Don't make me say it again" about 100,000 times in our childhood (she did, indeed, usually say "it" again). It was repetition that taught us to brush our teeth and hair before leaving the house, put our clothes in the hamper, and not leave our things strewn about the house. She did not love that kind of repetition, but it worked.

In order to change your mind, to adjust your thinking, you are going to have to repeat yourself *to* yourself. Since most of your present thoughts are the same ones you focused on yesterday, you will have to make a conscious effort to repeat your good thoughts to replace the negative thoughts. Every time one of the negative ideas you are used to entertaining sneaks back in, it is your job to chase it out (yet again) with the replacement thought.

When you put effort into memorizing something you repeat it over and over and over again. You read it, reread it, close your eyes, repeat it to yourself, check to make sure you got it right and then do it again. It is the same with these new thoughts, these new truths you are determined to install in your personal hardware. You must memorize the new thoughts, repeat them over and over and over again to yourself until they become your new normal. Doing this *is* annoying. It is not easy to install new hardware into yourself, to input new thought patterns. It is difficult, but it is well worth it. When you have a better thought life, you have a better life. The outcome is worth the annoyance.

Beyond installing new and positive thoughts, repetition also breeds belief. If you are currently battling feeling unworthy, not good enough, incapable etc. it is likely due to having been told these things repeatedly by someone or possibly yourself. Words have power but repetition has more. Repetition creates belief and when your beliefs are strong they trump anything said to you. This is true for positive *and* negative. When you believe the negative things that have been said to you, someone can say something kind one time and your mind likely will not believe it. The good news is that this works the other way too. When you believe positive things about yourself (because you have repeated these things over and over again), someone can criticize you or say something nasty and you will have the ability, the power, to let it roll off your back without internalizing that negativity.

Repetition = Belief

1 Minute Application: Repeat your new positive and true thought/phrase/sentence five times right now. (Schedule to do this everyday for the next five days.)

Ultimately, we are in control of our thoughts, our subconscious mind and our feelings. It does not often feel like we are in control but that is because we are human. We may respond with anger when we do not intend to or want to express anger. Sometimes we experience sadness and cry over something that may not logically seem tear worthy. Occasionally, we may feel discouraged or inferior when we do not want to. This is human nature. It is our job and part of life, to build up and intentionally strengthen our minds so that we *are* in control of these things. It takes effort to not burst out in anger or allow someone's thoughtless words to dictate who we are.

It is not easy. Working on this is a lifelong process that will feel as though you will never reach the finish line. It is difficult, kind of weird and can be frustrating. Often I fail at it. However, the lesson rings true in my ears, head and heart. When I mess up (again, and again, and again) I know this is right, true and worthy of a good fight. While I may never officially reach the finish line, I am moving forward with every effort I give to it. Undoubtedly, I am stronger now than I was when I was 15 years old. If someone's words hurt me or speak a lie about who I am, I can confidently believe that these are only words. It was a lie, or a painful word, but it will not make it past my thoughts to seep into my subconscious mind or become a belief about myself. I am stronger than that now. And I hope you will be too.

Keep Growing:
>*Power of Positive Thinking* by Norman Vincent Peale
>*Change Your Mind* by Coy Wire
>*Think & Grow Rich* by Napoleon Hill
>*The Inside Out Revolution* by Michael Neill

Marine Corps B.R.A.T.

3. Values

"It's not hard to make decisions once you know what your values are." - Roy E. Disney

When I sat down to begin writing this book I felt a little lost. A webinar walked me through a brain dump. A system to spill out all of my thoughts onto paper and then organize them into categories that could become potential chapters. *Marine Corps B.R.A.T.* popped into my head and the title spoke to me. The title is usually the final step when writing a book so I was already getting ahead of myself jumping in with such a strong name. The Marine Corps always held a specific set of values to me, such as, freedom, competition, strength, loyalty, toughness, no-nonsense, go-the-distance, winning and whatever-it-takes. As I type these I realize those are not all things you might consider "values." You likely will not see an inspirational poster of a meadow of flowers on the wall of a classroom that says "toughness." Later, I realized, that some of these attributes were Marine Corps specific but many of them were specific to my dad. To me, my dad is the essence, the embodiment of a Marine.

If you are a "real" military brat this book might bother you. My dad got out of the Marine Corps when I was only five years old. Therefore, I did not "grow up" as a Marine Corps brat. We did not change schools and move across the country or the world every two years. My memory does not even contain any military housing or very much of those six-month stints when my dad was absent. If this was, or is, your life, I commend and thank you and your family. My family sacrificed, but yours sacrificed for our country for the long-haul. Thank you for being a true military brat. Own that title proudly!

While this description does not illustrate my own experience with the military, what actually constitutes a Marine B.R.A.T.? Is being a B.R.A.T. the military lifestyle or being raised by a parent of the United States Military? Either way, I am proud that my dad served, that our family served and I am owning the title. All that to say, I can google what the Marines stand for, but for me, their essence and values are embodied in my dad. These attributes that I thought depicted Marines, actually described my dad.

Recently I explained a situation to my dad where I refused to do something for fear of looking stupid. My husband, on the other hand, never considers that thought before he does something. My husband will calculate the risks and danger of an act but not the level of visual stupidity he may achieve. He just goes for it, looks like an idiot and I try to pretend he is not with me. My dad laughed and said I sounded like the fighter pilots from his military days. Their theory was, "Better to die looking cool than to be caught doing something stupid." Instantly I pictured Tom Cruise in Top Gun and wondered where my aviators were. While my dad was laughing at me and telling me I essentially have an arrogance disease, I owned it and thought, "well yeah, but at least I look cool"…I do not have a problem.

Looking cool is not a value. Well, I suppose it could be. If that is one of the core beliefs you are using to guide your life by, then you may need this chapter (and maybe a therapist) more than you realize. Looking cool can be important to me but it is not a *value*. However, toughness (or *grit*) and freedom are values I hold. The discussion of values can suggest a fluffy, soft, pie-in-the-sky topic. What is the point? Unless you are putting inspirational posters around your bedroom why does sorting this out matter to your life? Even after understanding the importance of this I have thought, "This is too hard and why does it matter? I have more important things to spend my time on." Maybe you also consider this is silly and useless. What is the point?

Business coach and author Christy Wright says, "When you are intentional about your core values, you increase your speed of decision-making, avoid costly mistakes, reduce your stress, and ultimately stay true to yourself….It's not what you believe; it's what you're going to do about it." Unless you enjoy lengthy and hesitant decision-making, costly mistakes, stress and a lack of understanding yourself, then you need to know your values!

The problem is, most of the time when we are challenged to uncover our main values we are handed a list of loaded words without definitions and instructed to pick a few that sound right. Boom, bing, bam, done. Paste those words on your walls with a nature scene behind them and you are golden. You did the homework, completed the task and now you, your team, your company, should memorize these words and the culture and attitude ought to change without anymore effort. Onward we go!

However, we all know this method does not work to change your attitude or your team's culture. This format lacks conviction and commitment to the loosely chosen values. Values do not have to be big, loaded, meaningless words. In fact, they should not be those things. Values are meant to be full of meaning to *you*. They are supposed to represent all that is important to you in your life.

Value:
1. The regard that something is held to deserve; the importance, worth, or usefulness of something.
2. A person's principles or standards of behavior; one's judgement of what is important in life.
   (Oxford Dictionary)

Author and business coach, Donald Miller emphasizes that a mission statement, or your core values, should be words that cause you to take action. They should not be big, business-y words or phrases that only sound good or appear to be meaningful. They must actually *be* meaningful to *you*. When you choose values that matter to you, that strike a cord deep in your soul, it gives you a sense of mission. A driving purpose behind what you do and who you are.

According to Christy Wright once you know your values, not only does decision-making get easier, but they also give you a measurement to determine if you are living your life out of those values. For example, if you claim that family is your top priority (i.e. you value your family above all else) but your actions do not support that statement (i.e. you are regularly accused of being a workaholic and are never home) then you either are not living out of your values or you made up values that sounded good but did not realistically line-up with who you are and what is truly important to you.

My husband and I wrote a goal program to help others create and set goals that drive them in the direction of their dreams. We had discussed writing this program for a long time and finally decided to commit one month to get up at 4:45am every day to get the course written. We did it. It did not even take as much work as we thought it would. It was simply a matter of setting aside the time at the beginning of the day when we both think clearest. It was not fun to get up at that time but it was certainly enjoyable to make progress on one of our dreams. We are professionals at alternating hitting the snooze button in the morning. The thought that kept me getting up at 4:45 was, "Am I living out of my values right now?" If I rose with the alarm then I could answer "Yes!" Writing this program to help other people is something I put high importance on, so yes, getting up to work on it was living out of my values. Hitting the snooze button was not living out of my values. This guiding question has helped me become more disciplined and focused on many things in my life. When I say *these* things are what I value and then test myself on a regular basis, it changes my choices, which changes my life.

Values are more than a list of positive attributes that we aspire to maintain. Whether you know it or not every day you are acting out of your values. If you are not doing this intentionally then you may be living out of a set of values that do not coincide with what is really important to you. Personally, not asking that question when the alarm clock goes off in the morning has me living out the value of sleep over productivity. Productivity and accomplishment are important to me and I want my life to reflect that. Although, living that way does not always come naturally. Most of us go about our day without realizing what our actions say about what we value. The truth is, your values are more than what you *do* and are not about who you *want* to be. Your values indicate who you *are*. Values are not morals. They are principles and qualities that are most important to you. When you are acting out of your values you are more fulfilled. When you are fulfilled you are more likely to reach for and accomplish your dreams, therefore living a more satisfying life.

Values are meaningless unless they change you, your attitude and your culture. Summarizing Donald Miller, your core values must come from your core. They have to give meaning to your life and actions. They absolutely must *matter* to you. It does not even matter what they are as long as they matter to *you*. Your values should give you a deep sense of purpose, meaning and drive, which will cause you to be a happier and even healthier person.

How do you get there? If you cannot go to a teacher supply store and pick up a few posters containing what you thought were your values, how do you discover them? Can I print out a list of "values" from the world wide web and circle the ones that sound good? Absolutely not. They must come from what is most important to *you*.

For example, I recently began learning more about the enneagram, an ancient personality assessment that breaks all of human nature into nine personalities. For those who are unfamiliar with this and have not already figured it out, I am an 8, the "protective challenger." Through Ian Cron's book *The Road Back to You* I am learning that many of our values can come from our personality. For example, I value freedom, possibly above anything else. For many years I thought this value came from being homeschooled, my dad being in the military and all the things associated with those. From age six onward when asked what I wanted to be when I grew up my answer was "Business owner." Being a business owner, to me, meant freedom.

As I study the enneagram I am finding that, while my history and childhood may have a lot to do with this value, my personality also craves freedom. My enneagram number reflects that I am actually wired to have a my-way-or-the-highway attitude. Good or bad, it is part of my make up to desire for freedom in every way. This value is engrained in me. When anything associated with this value comes up I get chills. When I discover this value being disregarded or taken away from someone it fires me up. The value of freedom burns inside of me. It gives me meaning, purpose and it drives me.

During my husband's MBA program, one class required a values exercise that we both found extremely helpful. This book is not meant to be a workbook so you will not get space to conduct the exercise here. However, I strongly encourage you to take 30 minutes to do this for yourself. If you are unsure of what you value most and you do not want to pick a collection of big, fluffy words, this activity is very helpful in discovering your personal values.

Step One: To clarify your top 3-5 values you will want to take some time to identify 2-3 peak moments in your life that left you feeling alive, happy and fulfilled. Try to focus on a specific memory and your specific experience in that moment. What caused your elated feelings? What were you doing, thinking and feeling that caused fulfillment? Where were you? Who was with you? Once you have identified these, thought through it, and written it down, take a moment to pinpoint some of the characteristics that define this memory that reveal what you value.

Here is a personal example: After 26 months of hard work and sacrifice, my husband and I paid off all $44,000 of our student loans. It was an incredible feeling, realizing that our sacrifice had not been in vain. This was not a small feat for us. It was about more than getting rid of debt and being financially responsible. It was about committing to a lifestyle of change. I want to change our family financial tree. I want to see our kids grow up with the understanding that to be financially responsible is to be free. It opens up the opportunity to bless others without having to worry about our own circumstances.

Characteristics: Accomplishment, freedom, burden removed, leaving a legacy

Step Two: Now we will go in the opposite direction and identify 2-3 moments in your life when you were very angry or frustrated. Try to focus on the specific moment, and your specific experience in that moment. What caused your frustrated feelings? What were you doing, thinking and feeling that led to this frustration? Where were you? Who was with you? After you have written this out, identify some characteristics that define each of these memories that reveal what you value.

Personal example: Upon entering high school I had two best friends that made the first year of high school all that I could have hoped. As we approached our sophomore year, things changed. I made additional friends and my two girlfriends did not like the way I split my time with them. Nasty rumors began to circulate about me that were untrue and hurtful, which attacked my personality and integrity. Until this point, I had been under the impression that these two girls were my best friends. Trust had been built, and I expected that conflict could be dealt with head on. The lies, rumors and lack of resolution, (even when confronted) resulted in burned bridges and failed friendships. It was a painful season of learning who and how to trust people that left me cautious when developing friendships with females for many years after.

Characteristics: Cautious with trust and vulnerability, integrity, loyalty, honesty

Previously I said your values should not be big, fluffy words, but you likely wrote some of those down in the characteristics you identified from your stories. You will also see some from my own. The difference is that instead of being just words, these specific words now have meaning behind them. There is a reason you chose these specific stories, highlights and lowlights from your life. They somehow shaped you. Shaped the way you think and feel. They caused these words or values to take root deep within you. Instead of these being "just words" they are now meaningful to you and you understand *why* they are meaningful to you. Now that you can see and visualize your own stories behind these words, they have weight and can guide your decision-making in the future. To repeat Christy Wright, "It's not about what you *believe*; it's what you're going to *do* about it."

Armed with your newfound values you can conquer the world. Do not think I am being dramatic here. Conquering the world is defined by you. Not literally conquer the whole world, but *your* world. You can live out of these values and stop feeling like you are scrambling to keep up with life. You can confidently make decisions for your time, money, skills, energy, resources, etc. based on these values. When you do that you will find an inner peace. You may be busy as anything but when you are busy with things that matter to you it does not drain you. Be busy with what matters. Be busy spending time at home with your family, chasing your dreams, studying your spouse, busting your butt at the office, volunteering your time to organizations that pull on your heartstrings, etc. Whatever it is, you will find peace, happiness and fulfillment living out of your values.

Keep Growing:

The Road Back To You by Ian Morgan Cron
Do Hard Things by Alex and Brett Harris
The Happiness Hypothesis by Jonathan Haidt
Start With Why by Simon Sinek

Marine Corps B.R.A.T.

4. Education

"If you are not willing to learn, no one can help you. If you are determined to learn, no one can stop you." - Zig Ziglar

"Once you stop learning, you start dying." - Albert Einstein

"Education is the kindling of a flame, not the filling of a vessel." - Socrates

My mother-in-law has seven brothers, six living, and attending the southern family reunion every three years. They were raised as pastor's kids on a dairy farm and grew much of their own food in order to feed the family of 13. This family has stories from childhood that keeps the laughter going for days. Despite their financial situation and only having one bathroom, this family experienced immense joy and love growing up. Amazingly enough, 10 of the 11 children graduated college.

My first experience with this family, that now consists of over 100 people (those 10 got married, had children, who had children, and so on...) was at a Howell family reunion. At the time I was 19 and had been dating my soon-to-be husband for six months. This southern family opened their big hearts to me. They did not ask embarrassing or probing questions but simply wanted to get to know the newest stranger in their midst. While all six brothers look nearly exactly alike to me, I believe it was Uncle Jerry who caught me in the dining hall after dinner just before a round of games. He asked me, "What school are you going to?" To which I replied, "Oh just a community college near home in Pennsylvania." This sweet southern man in a crowded dining hall leaned closer to me, looked me in the eye and said, "Don't say *just* a community college. It's school and it's a smart place to go."

Since graduating high school I had gotten used to giving this answer, not even offering the name of Delaware County Community College because nobody outside of eastern Pennsylvania knew the school. Also, I was under the impression that attending a "community college" was less than remarkable or even interesting. Most people would nod their head at me and move to the next question since they either could not relate, did not know what to say or did not like my answer. Nevertheless, Uncle Jerry made me think about my answer. Community college was the right choice for me, for my family, for my finances, and my overall situation. However, this was the first time I did not feel inferior for giving that answer.

Both middle children in my family, my younger sister and brother, took a gap year after high school before going on to the next thing. I am immensely jealous of their wise choice and would change that about my path if I could go back. On a call with my brother one day early into his "gap" year he told me of a common interaction he was having with adults. It seems that no adult knows what to say when conversing with a graduating senior. Therefore, they resort to the standard "Where are you going to school?" 90% of the time they do not consider asking simply "What's next?" but assume that school is your next step. What else could there possibly be? Clearly that is the "correct" next step for every American high school graduate.

My sister, being the drama-queen of the family and sassy as she is, would either answer the standard question with the name of a different school each time, or said that she would be joining the circus. Yes, she actually said these things. Often. To adults. She's got nerve and a straight-face that can make it work. My brother's standard answer became, "Oh I'm taking a gap year. I will still be living at home." That last part to fend off the follow-up question, "Where will you live?" He lamented to me that often the response to him was, "Oh! Well that's ok!" To which he said, "This response has me beginning to think that it's not actually ok!"

Maybe you have experienced the feeling of adults looking down on your decision to do something different from the cultural expectation. Or maybe you did what was expected of you and now you regret it. Or possibly, you did what was expected and love where it has led you. Whichever path, I'm here to say that *education* is meant to be "the act or process of imparting or acquiring general knowledge, developing the powers of reasoning and judgement, and generally preparing oneself or others intellectually for mature life." (<u>dictionary.com</u>)

Rather than leaving 12 years of school feeling grateful, empowered, educated and privileged the typical U.S. high school graduate is breathing a sigh of relief that they made it through this period of forced "learning." Now, as a diploma-wielding 18 year old it is "Look out world, I am done learning!" Is that what school is? Is that what it was ever meant to be? A jail to store our children for so many hours a day, force-feeding them information they do not care about and will not necessarily help them in the "real world?" Are we calling this "learning" only to leave students with the aftertaste that learning is no fun? I think our great philosophers and founding fathers would be disappointed in this result.

Quick basic history lesson on education in America: Once upon a time children were primarily taught at home by their parents. Before the age of industrialization the provision of formal schooling was scarce. The goal of parents was to teach their children to read, write and understand basic math principles (arithmetic). The thought was, if you could do these three things, learn these three skills, you would be equipped to make it in life. In fact, most slaves and servants did not get this much education therefore, if you received the three basics you were already a step ahead. The "rich" folks in the 1800's would often hire tutors who would come to the house daily or live in the home with the pupils and their parents. Communities that could collectively afford to hire a teacher and build a schoolhouse (think *Little House on the Prairie* or *The Waltons*) did so, thus creating the one-room-schoolhouse concept. This set-up allowed for one teacher to instruct a group of students of all ages and skill levels at one time. The benefit was that there was no ageism. Children could learn from one another and the teacher had the freedom to flow from one subject to the next without restrictions on what must be taught when and for how long. By 1918 all American children were required to attend elementary school and hence, the system continued to grow into what it is today.[2]

An article found on businessinsider.com stated, "Schools in the U.S. have changed a lot over the years. Chalkboards have been updated to whiteboards and Smart Boards. Notebooks and textbooks have been replaced with laptops and iPads. Segregation was overturned by the Supreme Court, and students are demanding safe schools free of gun violence from today's lawmakers." This article provided pictures of classrooms from 1942 to 2018 to prove their point. It has been said that if Rip Van Winkle woke up today the only thing he would recognize would be the school system. Yes, segregation and gun laws were changed, but they were not changed *for* the school system. They were nationwide social and cultural changes which happened to *include* schools. These were not changes in our system for education but rather, our society. A whiteboard and a computer might stump old Van Winkle but the system for learning would be familiar. We have progressed to where we have computers in our pockets

---

[2] *Note: whether public, private or charter this is the path the school/educating children format has taken in the United States.

yet, we continue to teach our children in the same format as they did in the 1800's.[3]

In his book *Dumbing Us Down*, award winning teacher, John Taylor Gatto says this about our schools:

> "Look again at the seven lessons of school teaching: confusion, class position, indifference, emotional and intellectual dependency, conditional self-esteem, and surveillance. All of these lessons are prime training for permanent underclasses, people deprived forever of finding the center of their own special genius. And over time this training has shaken loose from its original purpose: to regulate the poor. For since the 1920s the growth of the school bureaucracy as well as the less visible growth of a horde of industries that profit from schooling exactly as it is, has enlarged this institution's original grasp to the point that it now seizes the sons and daughters of the middle classes as well. Is it any wonder Socrates was outraged at the accusation he took money to teach? Even then, philosophers saw clearly the inevitable direction the professionalization of teaching would take, that of preempting the teaching function, which, in a healthy community, belongs to everyone."

---

[3] *Note: Please understand that this is concerning the educational *system*. *Not* the teachers. Most teachers become such in an effort to help children and make a difference. Unfortunately, they often find themselves in positions that can feel more like a warden of a jail cell than an educator. I have the utmost respect for the individuals that work hard to educate children within the stifling boundaries set before them.

It does not have to be this way. Our school system does not have to continue to resemble something that was established in the 1800's. With the technology, research, and understanding we have today our system for educating children *should* be different. The biggest concern with the system in place is that students depart from it lacking a love for learning. They often graduate feeling relieved and free from something that was forced on them rather than gratitude for the privilege of being educated and for the men and women who taught them. The school system should spur an attitude of curiosity, a love for reading and exploring, offer the bandwidth to delve into subjects that interest individual students and the ability and opportunity for them to make their own wise choices after graduation.

My parents opted to homeschool all four of us from the beginning. They homeschooled not because they think the public schools they both attended are evil, or to shelter us from the reality of the world, but because they felt it was their responsibility as parents. Not every parent feels this way and that is okay. Many parents do not have the margin or the desire to educate their children. It does not make someone a bad parent and if you attended school (in any format) it does not mean you got gypped. It was my parents' personal conviction that homeschooling was the best way they could raise their own children to become responsible, respectful, self-sufficient and independent adults.

The decision to homeschool was not easy. On more than one occasion a well meaning woman has said to my mother, "I wish we had the means for me to stay home." Often, being a "stay-at-home-mom" was viewed as a luxury, something we could "afford." Rather, it was a choice to sacrifice and live on one income to prioritize what was important to my parents (something we can all do a little more of...prioritizing what is important to each of us). While my mom was trained as a teacher she quickly learned that homeschooling was completely different from a classroom setting. Not only did they have to learn *how* to homeschool their offspring but they were choosing to have all four of us at home ALL. THE. TIME. They had to learn how to select the right curriculum (or combination of curricula), for each very different child, who were all at different stages of learning, with different interests. They did not choose this because it was easy, but because for them, for us, it was right. And it was hard. Homeschooling gave us a gift of freedom for when we needed to move across the country without the move completely disrupting our lives.

Homeschooling is not for everyone. Certainly do not choose to homeschool simply because it is difficult, a challenge, to say the least. The message of this book is not to do things just because they are hard. Your kids may be in a public school (or the like) and they may be thriving; allowing you the space you need to be a better parent, or the opportunity to make the income necessary for your lifestyle. Or you may have been sent to school and did not know there were other choices. You are not a bad or less than parent or student because of any of this. What I want to impart is that there *are* options.

What is important are the lessons learned beyond the text-book and classroom. Lessons like learning how to think for yourself, how to find answers, how to learn and share with others (i.e. teach). Not all homeschoolers learned these concepts and not all public school students missed out on them. However, too many students (from every type of schooling) are graduating without these key ingredients for success. The adjustment behind our method of education needs a re-framing; a refocus on the *why* behind the schooling. Why do we require children to attend school for 12 years? Is it for easy daycare? To keep them "out of trouble?" What is the end goal for our children and do we need to rethink or re-structure how we educate them in order to achieve that goal?

However you were schooled as a child, or are educating your own children now, there are a few life lessons around education that I believe we should all keep impressed upon our minds and hearts. These concepts, in my humble opinion, are what the goal, the focus of educating our children should be centered around. The baseline of knowledge that our students should graduate understanding.

1. You Will Never Know All the Words

At age eight my mom realized I had been telling people I did not know how to read. Kids are funny and cannot be trusted. I was *that* kid. My parents and our home-life were allowed no secrets. Of course, being homeschooled already made me a little weird to others, but now I was saying I could not read and causing some people to raise an eyebrow at my mom.

She pulled me aside one day and asked why I was telling people I still could not read. We had gone through the book and I could read very well! My answer, "Because Mommy, I don't know *all* the words."

Oh, the embarrassing moments my mom endured, but they resulted in humorous stories. She gently explained to me that I will never know *all* the words but understanding how to sound out words and look them up meant that I could, indeed, read. Oh! Lightbulb moment for little Kylee.

Being homeschooled, every test or exam was open book be-cause...well, who was going to stop me? Upon moving to Pennsylvania we started utilizing cyber charter schools. This meant we were loaned computers, books and curriculum for our schooling and had access to teachers online. This freed my mom up and gave her a little bit of relief about home-schooling into high school. Cyber school took me from 8th grade through graduation. Being the type-A, organized child that I was, I enjoyed the structure of this system while it still gave me most of the freedoms of traditional homeschooling. However, I experienced an ethical struggle when it came to tests and exams. Everything was online, in my bedroom, at my own computer, with the books sitting beside me. Noth-ing stated open or closed-book but I felt I ought to know it all. That is the first time I remember my mom explaining to me that it is not about knowing everything, but knowing how and where to find the answers.

At this point I learned about the index in the back of a book, how to properly take useful notes, employ a highlighter and the great big world of Google (although I think 'Ask Jeeves' was the search engine at that time). It is not about memorizing every date, name, story and formula. It is about knowing how to find the answers and knowing how to learn.

This lesson may be the most important thing I learned in my entire school career. Although, I did not learn it thoroughly at that very moment, as any lesson takes repetition and time to steep. My mom had to repeat this concept to me many times for those last five years of school as I struggled to embrace and understand it.

"The trouble with our way of educating is that it does not give elasticity to the mind. It casts the brain into a mold. It insists that the child must accept. It does not encourage original thought or reasoning, and it lays more stress on memory than observation." - Thomas Edison

You will never know all the words. You will never have all the answers. You can however, learn how and where to find the answers. Even then, you may learn a great deal only to find you forget some things. Your brain can only hold so much. Even Sherlock Holmes did not know the basics of the solar system, for the sake of only keeping useful things in his mental hard drive, rather than filling his mind with all kinds of rubbish. [4]

---

[4] *This is not to imply that you should ignore information about our solar system.

Education ought to be the act of learning *how* to learn not a routine of memorization, exam, information dismissal.

You will never know all the words, but learn how to find the answers and the world is your oyster.

2. Self-Educate

"A formal education will make you a living; self-education will make you a fortune." - Richard Branson

"Imagine if schools actually helped kids identify their strengths by exploring their talents from a young age and growing their skills over the 12 years instead of letting them all follow the same routine and leaving them confused in life after graduation." - @Talliedar
The cyber school I participated in for high school provided me with a class catalog and transcript requirements. I was free to take any classes from the catalog, in whatever order I preferred, and I would be free to graduate when I met the transcript requirements. Educational freedom at its finest!

For science I took a sports medicine class and a forensics class. Having been given the freedom to skip art and music classes…I took advantage of it! By that point I was very, certain that I was uninterested and bad at those two subjects. With three credit requirements for math I opted for business math, practical math and pre-algebra. It is a little scary putting that in writing but it is the truth. Without a requirement on me to take any form of algebra, statistics, geometry or any of those other hateful things, I simply didn't, and also did not indulge anyone in that secret until just now. It has always felt like a secret, something I have rarely told anyone because of the anticipated judgement I felt I would receive for such things. It seems that people immediately jump to conclusions about my intelligence because I opted out of certain math courses required for most high school students. Math was not my strong suit and can confidently say, 10 years post-high-school, my adult life has not suffered by the absence of those classes. This should be good news! If your student is not great at math either, he/she will not die and will likely be able to live as a successful, self-sufficient adult without algebra!

Another controversial phenomenon from my high school days concerning my education: I took one class at a time. Yes, just one. Focusing on one class each day, for a two-three week timeframe allowed me to focus, to really learn the material and knock out classes quickly. Not five different courses for an hour each and every day. My mind does not work best that way. Focus for short periods of time is where I excel. No one cared how I got the work done as long as it got done and I learned in the process.

I have heard people argue that "kids" (you know, those teenagers who, 100 years ago were given tremendously more freedom and responsibility at that age...) should not be given as much freedom as I was given. Instead, we limit their freedoms until they turn 18, graduate, and then offer the world to them potentially ill-equipped to navigate it wisely. Turns out, teenagers are capable of far more than we give them credit for, if only we would allow them the freedom and responsibility to grow in those ways.

Having been given control of my own education at a young age, I learned the art, or skill, of self-education. If I was going to learn a concept, get the grade and attain the credit, it was up to me. I was too old for my mom to sit beside me all day and she had three other younger kids to teach. I had been given the tools I needed to learn, the rest was up to me.

Early into my married life I sat at a table outside a Starbucks leaning over a book with a highlighter in hand. An older gentleman walking into the shop commented "I am so sorry you have to be studying on such a nice day." I smiled at him as he disappeared through the door and thought to myself, "What a shame it is that he thinks a book and highlighter equal required studying rather than elected self-development." For indeed, I was reading for pleasure. Reading of my own volition. Highlighting because sometimes things ought to be highlighted and given special attention.

Since graduating high school I have learned more about who I am, what I think, what my skills and talents are and what I am capable of. From a very young age I expressed my desire to graduate high school early. My parents were always perplexed by this because they certainly had not put that thought or expectation into my head. They wanted me to be a kid as long as was appropriate. Play sports for four years of high school and enjoy that brief season of life. However, I wanted to be ahead. So goes the story of my life, always wanting to be ahead of where I am. Upon asking me why I wanted this early graduation I remember replying, "So that I can learn what I want to learn." As I recall that story I am amused and slightly in awe of that answer that came from a kid. Even then I understood the shackles of "required" schooling. There were so many more books to read and things to learn than what I was being offered "credits" for and I longed for the freedom and time to be able to study on my own.

Unfortunately, most graduate high school or college and call it quits on learning. They completely missed out on the joy of learning. It was squelched by the force-fed topics required of their degree or diploma. Too many adults relate the word "education" to a government system or building. Education is so much more. It does not end at a certain age or season any more than developing your intellect for a mature life ends when you turn 18.

Choosing to self-educate opens you to a world far beyond the information you were offered in school. Chase after it. Sit at a coffee shop with an open book and a highlighter. Take in more information that the world has to offer. Relish in historical stories and past lives lived. Discover the prized skills of people you long to emulate. Teach yourself how to juggle or do magic tricks simply for the joy of knowing how it is done. Whatever it is, find something that interests you, something you care about, and keep learning!

3. Read

"The man who does not read has no advantage over the man who cannot read" - Mark Twain

"The more that you read, the more things you will know. The more that you learn, the more places you'll go."
   - Dr. Seuss

"If you are going to get anywhere in life you have to read a lot of books." - Roald Dahl

In 4th grade I was proud to find out that I was at a 6th grade reading level, a trend that continued through grade school. In my ongoing quest to always be "ahead," whatever that meant for a given situation, this above average reading level satisfied my craving for achievement even while not understanding the purpose of a reading level. The year I was nine I read 100 books. I was nine…most of these were short, children's chapter books. Nonetheless, it was a goal I had set for myself and achieved. In fact, I believe I beat that goal again the next two years. I *loved* to read. It was rare to see me without a book. I could be caught reading in the car, in a waiting room, at a sibling's practice, or a brief moment when Mom got caught up in a conversation. At that age it was story books or historical biographies, delving into someone else's world, in a different time, and seeing things from their point of view. Age-appropriate biographies on Abraham Lincoln, Betsy Ross, Harriet Tubman and all kinds of people from our country's history fascinated me. Dry as they might be, they were real people's stories, people who impacted our nation.

One of my mom's main goals in homeschooling was to ensure we all loved to read and loved to learn. Whatever we learned in our "school age" with her was acceptable, but those were her two primary goals for our overall education. She knew if she could instill these traits in us that they would carry us through life. These traits would enable us to know how to find the answers and continue to grow for a lifetime.

The third kid, my oldest, younger brother, hated to read. It was like pulling teeth to get him to read anything. In the same way that Mom and I would both end up in tears doing math, the two of them would end in tears trying to get him to read. She purchased dozens of books trying to find something he would enjoy: superheroes, Star Wars, learn-to-draw, cars, cowboys, indians, dogs, outdoor themes, swords, guns, anything she could find. He was not interested. This carried on through his graduation. Then a miracle happened. The kid realized he needed to read in order to get where he wanted to be in his career and life. He was interested in real estate, as well as YoungLife ministry which involved daily dealings with people. Suddenly he began inhaling books. Spending hours a day (during that gap year) reading! Not storybooks, nothing fictional, only material that helped him learn, grow and move him towards his dreams and goals.

Storybooks, novels and fiction certainly have their place in reading; before bed to lose one's mind in a story, on the beach or a place of relaxation. These books allow us to imagine and dream. They fuel our imagination and allow us to be creative, a feat difficult for adults to retain once they have surpassed childhood. It is amazing what your subconscious mind can do while lost in a story. Have you ever been reading something light, a story, and a profound thought pops into your mind? When the subconscious is given a moment to relax it concocts all kinds of useful thoughts. It is a good practice to always be in the middle of a novel even though it may not be read every day.

A dear friend and mentor said, "As a leader and business-owner, the nonfiction you read should always outweigh the amount of fiction you read." At that point you could usually find me in one of each on any given day. Two books going at once. Since then, my non-fiction outweighs the fiction two or three to one. And I have learned so much. The "books to read" list on my phone is eternally growing. Buy me books for Christmas, that's all I want. Recently, I read three books on the art of speed reading with the intent to be able to read more books in a shorter amount of time. There are *so* many useful and recommended books and I want to read them all!

Can you believe the nerve of Mark Twain? Saying that one who chooses not to read is no better, has no advantage over the one who cannot? To my knowledge, I have never met an adult who cannot read. Being unable to read, I imagine, must feel like driving on a road in a country where you do not know the language. You can see the letters, you know they are words, but you have no idea what they are trying to communicate to you. Signs all around and yet you can be hopelessly lost.

We all know that the ability to read has not always been expected of the general population. Today this skill is recognized as fundamental to succeeding at anything in life. While I might not be able to name an adult who cannot read, I have met many who choose not to. When someone tells me they do not read, do not like to read, or do not have time to read, I am shocked and saddened by it every time! There is so much to learn, knowledge to gain and growth to come from reading and you are telling me you are uninterested? Instantly I feel sorry for all you are missing.

Upon moving to Rhode Island, I was invited to a book club by a new acquaintance. She said I was welcome to attend the upcoming gathering even though I had not read the book. Arriving, I quickly realized the book they were discussing was fiction. This baffled me. The only book clubs I had ever participated in were concerning non-fiction or specific studies. What was the point of discussing a fictional story? Where was the growth to be obtained? My previous understanding was that these gatherings were to share impact, revelations and encourage personal growth. What convicted or challenged you within these pages? How was this read going to change you for the better? How can any of that be done with a fictional read?[5]

---

[5] *Fictional book clubs can certainly appeal to and even fulfill some individual's needs. However, it is not my cup of tea and that is okay.

While books have the power to free you from a situation by taking your mind away to a story, they also give you the power to self-educate. To learn whatever you want on your own time. Reading gives you the opportunity to study whatever subject interests you, areas in which you would like to grow or new information you would like to obtain. Today, you can find dozens of books on any topic with a few clicks of a button, and the new book can often be on your porch in less than 24 hours or even downloaded in the moment. Fortunately we have the gift of choice. Outside of our standard schooling it is up to each person whether they will choose to read and to self-educate on the things that matter to them. Unfortunately, most were never taught to adore reading or to understand the power in self-education beyond classroom walls. Rarely, if ever, in a traditional school system are you encouraged to read what interests you, at your own pace and then report back on how it impacted you. Books give us power and freedom for our entire lives.

Whatever education you received or your own children are receiving now, you still get to make this choice. The love of reading can be learned no matter your age, education level or type. The ability and desire to read gives you freedom, but also power. Reading puts your mind and your education into your own hands. You get the choice to read or not to read, to read this book or that, to grow and excel in an area of importance to you or not. The choice is yours and the books are waiting.

4. Think

"Children must be taught *how* to think, not what to think."
- Margaret Mead

"The book to read is not the one that thinks for you but the one which makes you think." - Harper Lee

"Education is not the learning of facts but the training of the mind to think." - Albert Einstein

Texas in the summertime is *hot*. One day, with my dad out of town, my mom was vacuuming the pool in a hot pink, midriff tank top, hair thrown into a banana clip, with four kids and two dogs running around the yard. Suddenly, she realized she was supposed to be at a focus group meeting at the library. She had been specifically invited by the children's librarian to attend the meeting concerning the new library building and organization thereof. I cannot even remember what she did with us, but she dropped everything and got herself there just in time. A sweaty, thrown-together mess who had just spent the afternoon in the Texas heat vacuuming a pool. Although embarrassed by her appearance it did not stop her from putting some people in their place that day. In Texas, there is a large population of conservative homeschool families and this particular meeting consisted of several local homeschooling moms with a little too much conservatism on their hands. It almost hurts me to say that priding myself as a fierce conservative. But these women needed to chill. They got a bit hysterical about the organization of the library books and said that they ought to "Separate the *good* books from the *bad* books." My mom was that poor librarian's back-up as they both sat there, shocked by what they were hearing. One woman in particular shared a story about an instance with her daughter when they were looking for a book on a specific topic and (because of the Dewey decimal system) the young girl stumbled across a book on witchcraft. The mother was horrified, shoved the book out of view and refused to answer any of her daughter's questions concerning the "unmentionable" book. My mom piped in, "You just missed out on a teaching opportunity! What greater way to teach your daughter your views of right from wrong or about any subject than by her coming across it in real life and asking *you* about it? When our children cannot come to us with their questions you better believe they are going to go to someone else." Clearly, my mom's vote was to stick with the standard way of organizing the library books; "good" and "bad" all together!

Many people assume that parents homeschool in an effort to shelter their children from the world. This way they can feed them exactly what it is they want them to hear, learn, do and say. To create miniature robots of their version of perfect human beings. One of my mom's dearest, longest friends said that, upon meeting our family and learning that we homeschooled, she immediately assumed we were "mushroom children." As she warmed up to us and we proved not to be complete weirdos she shared this first impression with my mom. "What are mushroom children?!" My mom asked with big, confused and concerned eyes. "You know, like mushrooms. They're grown in sheltered darkness and fed shit!"

These assumptions about homeschooling could not be further from the truth about our particular experience. We were given freedom to question everything and a safe space to discuss it. Consistently challenged to develop our own opinions and thoughts, and if our parents did not have answers to our questions, we were encouraged to seek out those answers on our own. Instead of being told to "get good grades" our parents said, "Are you learning?" They cared less about our grades as long as we were putting in our best effort and learning the information. In high school I read *The Shack*, an excellent story that challenged my perspective. Only recently did I discover it is not normally recommended for a teenager. This book challenged my mindset and opinions on God. It reminded me that I know next to nothing, to not take myself too seriously and to not limit God. He's God. While critics came against the book for being unbiblical, I took away a new mindset and perspective. Instead of hearing critics' opinions and claiming them as my own, I had been encouraged to dive into things of question and form my own thoughts. In essence, to think for myself and decide what I believe without being swayed by others.[6]

My dad handed me *Rich Dad Poor Dad* by Robert Kiyosaki when I was 16 and my mind was opened to a new perspective on learning. While my parents had instilled a desire in

---

[6] *Note: not all homeschoolers have these same experiences and not all students in a standard school system missed out on this or any of these lessons. This is simply my own experience and lessons I believe are worth sharing.

us to learn, this author challenged me to seek out jobs and positions in life in which I would learn a new trait or skill. To value the lesson learned over the money earned. The kind of books and conversations we were constantly surrounded by challenged us to use our brains. Challenge our thinking and ask ourselves "Why do I think this way?" My parents never forced us to be anything, but encouraged us to challenge and question everything.

Most of the time I see this lacking in schools (homeschools too). Rather than being encouraged to ask questions and challenge answers, children are often taught to memorize the "correct" answers to pass the test and please the teacher, administrators or state officials. Obviously, some dates, names and formulas must be memorized. Those clearly have "right" answers. What about everything else? Too often, teachers are on a time crunch, wrangling students, attempting to teach them something before their time is up. They are not given the time or opportunity to answer hard questions or to entertain new thoughts when they are required to complete specific material in only 45 minutes. Most teachers pursued a teaching career in an effort to make a difference, not to wrangle kids and kill their joy of learning because they have to follow the rigid map laid out for them.

One example of this is from *Rich Dad Poor Dad*. The premise of the book dives into a mode of thinking that is, frankly, grossly outdated and yet still lives in the minds of many, if not most adults. The concept of parents telling their kids to go to school, get good grades, so they can then find a "safe" and "secure" job. Everything about this is wrong for today's job culture and yet, it is still taught and encouraged because that is what "they" (many of our parents and teachers) were taught. Teachers work hard to help their students get good grades and yet there is no correlation between those grades and becoming a happy, thriving, "successful" adult in the real world. We now have generations that have been taught this way. It has come to the point that we have an entire cultural belief system that claims you cannot "get ahead," be "successful," or be worth much of anything if you do not graduate college. Case-in-point: the responses my siblings and I received after high school graduation when we shared that we were not going to a four-year-college. Then, those that do follow the path laid out for them have been led to believe that a "good" job ought to be handed to them because they did, indeed, follow the yellow brick road that someone paved for them.

This thinking that has been passed down multiple generations and is not only wrong for today's generation, culture and time, prevents independent thinking. Being told "This is the right way" at a young age by people children trust and respect, we squelch their ability to wonder, "Is there another option?" Unless parents and teachers are handing children books or telling them stories of those that did not excel in school, did not get good grades or did not follow the yellow brick road who have "made it," they will never know to ask. If we do not allow children to wonder, explore, ask and challenge (yes parents, even challenge your way of thinking) then they will simply follow the path and never learn to think for themselves. An education ought to challenge the mind, not tell it what to think.

5. Teach

My husband *loves* to learn. He loves the classroom setting, group projects, writing papers, student discussions, etc... Six months into marriage, he graduated with his bachelors degree and I was honing in on the final semester for my associates degree, when he began talking about getting his M.B.A. Hanging on by a thread financially and knowing that the student loan bills were coming soon, I bucked the idea, assuming he wanted that degree because it was just the next "thing." I thought because society may have planted an idea in him that made him think he needed that additional degree. However, in his wisdom and patience, he kept working the idea on me. At great lengths we discussed why he wanted that degree, how it would benefit him and us and the purpose of it. I wanted to be absolutely certain that he wanted the degree because *he* wanted it, not because someone told him he "needed" it. Three years later he did go back, because this guy loves to learn. He truly did not care about the degree, the piece of paper, but felt he would learn more that he could directly apply to his work and our business. He was right. He went back for his M.B.A. and his company covered the cost (much to my satisfaction). He has used so much of that experience in his work and our business and even I learned from his time back in school.

Learn to learn. Do not ever let the completion of school stop you from learning. My husband is a student of life. Read books, attend conferences and seminars, dive into difficult conversations, challenge the way others think and let them challenge you. Discuss to learn not to defend. And teach.

66

Marine Corps B.R.A.T.

Teach what?

You do not have to be a "teacher" to teach. The one who learns the most is the person doing the teaching or the speaking. When you teach a subject you learn the material thoroughly. My husband would employ this tactic with school projects. He would ask if he could teach me about what he was learning. Instead of memorizing the information, when you teach you have to coherently regurgitate information. You must know your material in order to answer questions or help someone who may not comprehend. It is the process of helping someone else to learn.

> "School failed me, and I failed the school. It bored me. The teachers behaved like Feldwebel (sergeants). I wanted to learn what I wanted to know, but they wanted me to learn for the exam. What I hated most was the competitive system there, and especially sports. Because of this, I wasn't worth anything, and several times they suggested I leave. This was a Catholic School in Munich. I felt that my thirst for knowledge was being strangled by my teachers; grades were their only measurement. How can a teacher understand youth with such a system? From the age of twelve I began to suspect authority and distrust teachers." - Albert Einstein

As long as you continue to learn, to self-educate, you will always know something someone else does not. You will always have something to teach. Not in a self-righteous, pompous way, but in a compassionate, caring way. Be aware of what you know and how you can help others with your knowledge. Teach to share, assist, improve, not to measure, judge, or direct. This is the heart of teaching.

Not all homeschooled kids were taught these five lessons about education and learning. Not all standard classroom kids missed out on them. It is my belief that these are the true keys to success, however you want to define success, whether by the "American Dream" or a completely different metric. You cannot lose as long as you recognize that:

1. You will never know it all, but you can find the answers.
2. Your education is never really over, and you have the power to learn anything and everything you desire.
3. Reading is the cornerstone of learning.
4. Thinking for yourself and challenging thoughts (your own and others) gives you the strength and courage to speak with conviction.
5. Teaching is the most thorough and generous way to gain knowledge and wisdom.

Keep learning. Keep growing.

"If we encounter a man of rare intellect, we should ask him what books he reads." - Ralph Waldo Emerson

"It is what you read when you don't have to that determines who you will be when you can't help it." - Oscar Wilde

Keep Growing:

Dumbing Us Down by John Taylor Gatto
Weapons of Mass Instruction by John Taylor Gatto
Rich Dad Poor Dad by Robert Kiyosaki

Marine Corps B.R.A.T.

5. Entrepreneurship

"The goal isn't more money. The goal is living life on your own terms." - Chris Brogan

"Entrepreneurship isn't just a label - it's a lifestyle."
    - Richard Branson

"The entrepreneur always searches for change, responds to it, and exploits it as an opportunity." - Peter Drucker

Your dream may be to work for someone else your entire life and that is fine. There is another chapter in this book for the employees. However, if you have ever dreamed of owning a business, being completely in charge of your work or if you have been too scared to even allow yourself to think of such a thing, this chapter is yours.

Three pet peeves that make my skin crawl are:
1. When people use words they do not know how to say (example: "supposebly" instead of "supposedly," "pacific" instead of "specific," "libary" instead of "library," or "irregardless" instead of "regardless").
2. When my husband leaves cabinet doors open, or leaves empty, opened envelopes on the counter.
3. When people think they need a degree in order to start or run a business.

Marine Corps B.R.A.T.

A few years ago one of my mom's best friends asked her when I was going to get a "real" job followed by, "I can just see her running a company as a CEO or VP or something." While her children were doing the extended college life thing, I was working as a personal trainer, working with a reputable direct sales company, dealing black-jack and acting as an occasional house organizer for this particular family friend. These were not my lifelong aspirations by any means. However, in that season, my husband and I were broke new-lyweds attempting to make ends meet. While the income (or lack thereof) was not my favorite part of that particular season of life, the perk of the odd side jobs was that I was in control. It was up to me to say yes or no to a job and have control over my schedule. As a personal trainer, even when working for a gym, I set my own hours and when I left town I simply informed my clients and left. The core of my being runs on this kind of freedom.

When we moved to a new state I briefly worked as a receptionist for a salon and spa. It puzzled and irritated me when the boss told me I could not have two consecutive Saturdays off. Why did this bother me more than the other employees? I called my parents to share my latest revelation, "You guys made me a brat!" They hesitantly laughed at my accusation but also wondered what exactly I was blaming them for. As children, whenever we had an issue with my mom's parenting style her famous response was, "Tell your therapist about it when you're 30." I could sense that remark coming as I shared this revelation with them. I further explained, "I am addicted to freedom and control and it is making me a terrible employee." Freedom made me a brat. Although, I am better for it and oddly proud of it. Growing up with the kind of freedom we had as children made it difficult for me to relinquish that same freedom as an adult. We tend to think adulthood equals freedom. Adulthood provides many freedoms, but only if we choose to take hold of them. Most of the freedoms we are offered get tied down due to "cultural norms."

The biggest freedom we were blessed with growing up was that of time. Being homeschooled meant the schedule fluctuated. Some homeschoolers were more rigid with their schedule than we were. We did not really set alarm clocks, we could eat when we wanted, play outside when it was snowing, sunny or a perfect pool day. We went to the bathroom without permission, doctors appointments required no notes and we did school in cars, waiting rooms, treehouses, bunkbeds, gyms, churches, etc… We were taught in this way to *learn* rather than to *school*. When the military or a job relocated us, we picked up and moved. My parents did not have to concern themselves with popping us into a new school in the middle of a school year, which meant we could move whenever necessary. Some days we played catch up in the textbooks and on reading, while other days were dedicated to museums, libraries or science experiments. For a few years my grandmother rented a condo on the beach for us to enjoy for the entire month of September. After all the other kids had gone back to school and we could have the beach to ourselves! This lifestyle taught me that time is mine. I am given the same amount as everyone else, but I am completely in control of how I spend it. Even sitting in waiting rooms during my grandmother's chemo treatments, I could choose to spend that time pouting and irritated, working on schoolwork, a craft project or reading a book. The choice, the freedom to choose how I spent that time, was mine.

Unfortunately, most adults do not grasp this concept. They do not understand the freedom they have over the time they are given, much less any of the other freedoms at their disposal. Due to my upbringing I realized that I do not make a very good employee. The desire to get the work done well and on time, (like a good employee would) was there, but the discrepancy was on *when* that happened, I wanted it on *my* time. Not the time you say I have to work on it. It still puzzles me that employers would turn down a hard working, honest, candidate simply over *when* they get the work done.

From a very young age, when asked what I wanted to be when I grew up, my answer would be, "I want to own my own business!" Entrepreneurship has run in my blood since I can remember. The debacle over scheduling at the salon only solidified this in my mind and I have not worked for someone else in over four years.

The problem with these "cultural norms," with my mom's friend's question, is that the general population tends to assume that college or a degree equals success in career (*see also: success in life*).[7] This is not true. Get a secure job, do not make waves, be normal.

"No, no, no!
Stick to the stuff you know
If you wanna be cool
Follow one simple rule
Don't mess with the flow, no no
Stick to the status quo!"
      (Cue any *High School Musical* fans here)

These rules or assumptions limit adult freedoms. The "secure" job means working for someone else who controls your schedule, your income and the majority of your most limited and valued commodity, your time. Not making waves and being normal equals limits. However, not following this path means that you will experience naysayers. There will be odd looks and comments when you do not just "get a job." This is an alternative path, it is counter-cultural and uncommon. If you consider choosing an alternative path you are often viewed as if you have three heads or are just too young and ignorant to understand what you are doing.

My parents did not specifically tell us to challenge everything or go against the grain, but they modeled it by making choices or following paths that were difficult and often un-

---

[7] *College and a degree certainly *can* assist someone in experiencing success in a career. The problem is assuming that this is the only route to achieve success and also, assuming that "success" has only one definition.

usual. In high school I had a solid group of "schooled" friends (though maybe a little strange, certainly not the bottom of the clique food chain), while still being home-schooled. Well aware that I was not the coolest but at least I was not the un-cool-est. Since then, I think I have progressively gotten "un-cool-er" each year as I continue to challenge what "adulthood" is going to look like on me.

This was not necessarily my plan. Graduating high school with 12 college credits, I registered myself for a full fall class load at the local community college. Always on time, always turned in my homework and projects, never missed a class, and was definitely my Composition II professor's favorite student. And I hated it all.

My grand plan had always been to graduate high school early (which I did not do), attend college for business (which I did not do), then get a job to pay the bills while I started my own business (which I did not do). Isn't that what you were told to do too? Is that the direction your teachers, advisors, guidance counselors, and parents all encouraged you to go? My parents were "weird" and did not encourage that plan, they kind of shrugged and said "ok" to all my grand plans. That program was basically the status quo. The "normal" or "expected" route for me and anyone my age.

Maybe that is, or was, you too. You were told "This is the way to go" but along the way you hated it, realized that path was not for you and that you had to adjust your plans. Or maybe you hated it and still went along with it because you thought it truly was the map to "success."

Most people are not told this stuff. That you do not owe your boss anything. That you can find another job in another city, or another state anytime you want. That you can change positions or completely change careers. Nobody told you that you are completely in charge of your own future, that you can discover what it is you love to do and then go do it and get paid for it! Nobody told you that you do not *have* to go to a prestigious college, have a degree to get a certain job or even to start your own business. In fact, most of us are told precisely the opposite. Or at the very least, it is implied to us. However, there is so much more freedom available if we are willing to take hold of it. It has been said:

- "Follow your dreams or you'll spend the rest of your life working for someone who did." - Unknown
- "Build your own dreams, or someone else will hire you to build theirs." - Farrah Gray
- "Your salary is the bribe they give you to forget your dreams." - Unknown

Entrepreneurship is not for everyone. Not everyone wants to own a business, and that is okay. If you want to work for someone else and that gives you energy and happiness, then by all means do that! That is what this book is about, simply challenging the "norm" and living your life on *your* terms. That is what entrepreneurship has done for me and my husband. The problem is, too many people limit themselves and/or think they cannot do it, or simply do not have the confidence in themselves that they need. Let me just say this loud and clear:

YOU DO NOT NEED A DEGREE
TO BE SUCCESSFUL IN BUSINESS.

My dad said, "Own your own business, don't work for someone else." All of my childhood he instilled in us this sense of freedom.

Freedom:
1. The state of being free or at liberty rather than in confinement or in physical restraint.
2. Exemption from external control, interference, regulation, etc.
3. The power to determine without restraint.
4. Political or national independence.
5. Personal liberty as opposed to bondage or slavery.
6. Exemption from the presence of anything specified.
    (dictionary.com)

Freedom is being "at liberty," or "exemption from external control." Ahhh, music to my ears. Once, I worked as a personal trainer at a gym where the training manager preyed on the young female trainers. It was a bad situation, and as I cried on my drive home one day I realized, "I do not have to put up with this!" So I didn't. I found another job as a trainer and left that position. Not long after that I gathered enough private clients to be self-employed as a trainer working fewer hours and making more money. Most people would never bounce job to job this frequently. Obviously, if you are attempting to be a model employee you do not want to be viewed as a "bouncer." However, there is a common thought out there that when someone hires you, you then "owe" them a certain amount of time in that position. This is malarkey. An employer said, "We would like to utilize your skills and give you money for it." And you *owe* them for that? Absolutely not! If something better comes along two days later there are no rules that you cannot move on.

The general public assumes that security, good income, and happiness come from working 40 hours a week at a "safe" and "secure" job. We have taught children and conditioned brains to believe that our freedoms are limited. As a patriotic, red blooded American you will never verbally admit that you think your freedoms are limited. However, if you take a moment to analyze the way you think, talk, and act you may quickly recognize that either you really do believe this way. Or, you have succumbed to the brainwashing and settled into a life of limits. We have been told that business is hard and that most fail. Doing hard things is…well, hard. Why put ourselves out there and attempt something that most fail doing? Then, even if we feel up to the challenge of a business, most times we think degree = success. Therefore business degree = business success. Instead of getting started we enroll in school, putting off the business dream until later when we are "qualified." I did this. Starting school I thought I would get a business degree since "owning my own business" was all I had wanted to do since I was six years old. Then the math courses intimidated me and I changed majors to Communications. Finally finishing my Associates degree I never looked back. Do you know how much I use algebra in my daily, successful, adult life? Never. Luckily, I do not fret over how I never took those statistics or accounting classes in college. "Man, my life would be so much better if I had taken more accounting classes," said no one ever.[8]

This might be the very first time you have heard any of this before. If so, I am so sad you did not grow up with this knowledge, but I am also thrilled you are ingesting it now! Instead of honing in on good grades my parents shared with us every time they heard a business success story. In case you did not know, there are a ton of people who have established and run incredibly successful businesses before they had any idea what they were doing (and without college degrees). Here are few:

Television:
    Ted Turner (founder of CNN)
    Ellen DeGeneres (Ellen Show)
    Steven Spielberg (movie director)
    Walt Disney (ahem...Disney)
    Oprah Winfrey (Oprah show, magazine, etc.)
    Simon Cowell (music entrepreneur)
Fashion:
    Ralph Lauren (clothing line)
    Anna Wintour (Vogue Magazine)
Computers/Technology:
    Steve Jobs (Apple)
    Michael Dell (Dell)
    Bill Gates (Microsoft)

---

[8] *Disclaimer: proper accounting *is* important in any/every business, but you do not have to be an expert in accounting to own your own business. Go read a book or watch a YouTube video to figure it out, or delegate and hire an accountant!

Food:

      Colonel Harland David Sanders (KFC)

      Dave Thomas (Wendy's)

      Rachael Ray (media personality)

      Ray Kroc (McDonald's)

Vehicles:

      Henry Ford (Ford Motors)

      Soichiro Honda (Honda)

Communications:

      Anthony Robbins (motivational speaker and author)

      Joel Osteen (pastor of church with 40,000+ members)

      Scott Fitzgerald (writer)

Social Media:

      Mark Zuckerberg (Facebook)

      Jerry Yang (founder of Yahoo)

      Travis Kalanick (founder of Uber)

Inventors:

      Thomas Edison (inventor of the lightbulb and more)

      The Wright Brothers (inventors of the aeroplane)

      Albert Einstein (theory of relativity and more)

Politics:

      George Washington (first President of the United States)

      Abraham Lincoln (16th President of the United States)

Other:

      Benjamin Franklin (scientist, politician, artist, writer, philosopher, etc...)

      Richard Branson (founder of the Virgin Group)

      Milton Hershey (Hershey chocolate)

      John D. Rockefeller (oil tycoon)

Marine Corps B.R.A.T.

David Green (founder of Hobby Lobby)
John Mackey (founder of Whole Foods)
Mary Kay Ash (founder of MaryKay cosmetics)

Sometimes I can look at a list of successful people and think, "Yeah, but I'm not like them." Due to an almost unhealthy amount of confidence in myself I do not often have this thought. Although, I have experienced it, so I understand if that is where you are. For example, Steve Jobs, Bill Gates, Henry Ford, Mark Zuckerberg, these men have a specific kind of brain, a way of thinking, that I do not possess. They are successful business people and an excellent example but I am not going to find myself running a successful computer, coding, or car company. My brain does not function that way. However, that is why the list is so long. There are people in Every. Single. Industry. who have created success for themselves without a degree! Without having a clue what they were getting into! Without having it all mapped out! In fact, most of these people may have experienced more life trauma, been in more dire situations than you or I have or will ever experience, and they *still* made it work! Hence, you have lost your excuses. There is someone in your industry, or in the industry that you love and have a passion for, that has made it work. What are you going to do to make it work for you?

Did you know there has never been a better time in all of history than right now to start a business? Do you know that the widespread use of the internet and the smartphone has completely revolutionized how businesses run today? Did you know you can run a business from a laptop? Without an office, printer, fax machine or additional phone line? It is incredible! Full-fledged, successful businesses have been started with as little as $5 in this atmosphere! Every business is different, and putting a general number on the cost to begin a business is unfair. Nonetheless, according to Business News Daily, most micro businesses started today cost around $3,000 while a home based franchise costs $2,000-$5,000. While you may not have $2,000-$5,000 sitting in the bank ready to throw at starting a business, let's put this into perspective. In 1980 the most basic model of an HP 3000 home computer sold for $95,000. This is the equivalent of slightly over half a million dollars today (*USA Today*). If a computer is necessary to start a business, rather than needing $95,000 in 1980 (and remember, you had to know how to work those dinosaurs) you can get started in 2020 with anywhere from only $5 to $5,000!! Also remember, when that guy bought his $95,000 computer, the internet had not been invented yet! Whatever your hardship, your struggle, your upbringing, your lack of cash, knowhow, or expertise, I guarantee one of those successful entrepreneurs on the list had it worse. These stories are not only about success, they are stories of immense resilience, perseverance and overcoming hardships. These are people to look up to, not for their net worth or how society deems them "successful," but because of their persistence. Their endurance to chase after their dream in spite of naysayers and bumps in the road.[9]

---

[9] https://www.usatoday.com/story/tech/2018/06/22/cost-of-a-computer-the-year-you-were-born/36156373/

Business is the essence of freedom. It is not only the freedom to wake up or work whenever you want, or creating your own schedule and task list. It is taking your life and well being into your own hands. It is not relying on someone else for your income and livelihood. It is saying, "I have a dream, a passion, or skill that I believe will flourish in the marketplace. I am going to give it a fair shot and make this life my own." This can, at the same time, be paralyzingly scary and adrenaline junkie thrilling. It is not for everyone and certainly not for the faint of heart. However, it can be for you if you want it to be. Even if you did not grow up with parents who encouraged this, you have never thought about it until this moment, or God-forbid you do not have a business degree. Business and the freedom thereof can still be for you. Besides the freedom it offers there are a few things to know about business.

1. Business *is* hard.

Enjoying knitting is not a good enough reason to go into business. If you want to sell some of your homemade wares then have at it (a great resource for a small business in this capacity is etsy.com). However, to go into business there must be a greater push, a larger reason, your why for pursuing it. Even when you are in business doing something that you love there are bad days and days you do not want to do that thing you thought you loved. I love writing but there are days when I hit a wall, cannot form real sentences, and get irritated with the whole process. That does not mean I quit, that writing is not for me, or that the book is useless. It just means that some days are harder than others. When you experience those days you must have a deeper meaning, or purpose, behind what you are doing. *Why* you are in business will speak life into you and your organization on the tough days. Love what you are in business doing and be passionate for why you are in business doing it.

2. Business takes time.

Lori Greiner says, "Entrepreneurs are the only people who will work 80 hours a week to avoid working 40 hours a week." How is this freedom? Sounds to me like working twice as hard and long in a week is not exactly freeing....? Oh, but it is! When it is something you love and care for it is your baby, and you will do everything in your being to make it succeed. You have likely identified doting new parents who are exhausted. They are sleep deprived, they are at the newborn's every beck and call, completely out of touch with reality and the rest of the world. Yet, they would not have it any other way. They love that child so deeply that all their sacrifice is worth it. It is the power of love. Do you love your work that way? In recent years I have learned a little more balance in my life but there was a time when my husband and I had a free evening and he asked me, "What do you want to do?" With a sheepish grin I answered, "Work." I was so passionate about what I was doing that I did not want to rest, I wanted to keep pressing forward doing the work I cared so dearly about. This is entrepreneurship. It is working like a parent for their child, to keep them alive and help them be successful. It is when your business never leaves your mind completely. For some, they would rather do the job and go home, separate themselves from their work and receive the paycheck. Working this hard, pouring this much sweat equity and love into something that cannot guarantee success, may sound like a ball and chain, shackles rather than freedom. However, for those with the entrepreneurial spirit in them, these words feel like the freedom of a wild stallion. It feels like a breath of fresh air and letting your hair down.

We might work harder and longer and not have a clue what we are doing in this entrepreneur's journey, but having control over our time makes every bit of it worth it. We get to choose when and where we work, what the work is, and what is worth our focus and effort. That is freedom.

3. Business can be learned.

Just as Robert Kiyosaki teaches that sales is a necessary skill for every human to possess, business is a learned skill. Some are born with an entrepreneurial spirit. For some, entrepreneurship happens out of necessity or frustration. A baker opens their own shop because they are fed up with how other bakeries are run. Businesses have been started simply because someone thought, "I could run this place better than the owner." Others realize they need to make some extra money to make ends meet, and a hidden skill or hobby turns into a business. Businesses can be dreamt up, fall into your lap, be a resolution to a problem, or begin as a hobby you enjoy. Most business owners did not start out as a child saying, "When I grow up I want to own my own business!"

Disney is a household name in America and many parts of the world. Walt Disney is said to have had a net worth of about $1 billion at the time of his death in 1966. While we may view this man as a legend, a successful producer, director, screenwriter, voice actor, animator, entertainer, etc... not one of his dreams would have come true without his brother. While Walt had the imagination that created the magic of what we know as Disney, he did not have the know-how to bring his imagination to life. Like many artists or creatives, his follow through was lacking. Roy Disney, Walt's older brother, was the mastermind behind everything Walt created. Roy was the businessman, the finance guy, the entrepreneur, the behind the scenes role that made Disney. Upon being asked what would happen if Walt suddenly died, Walt said, "Absolutely nothing. My brother Roy runs this company. I just piddle around." Whether you recognize your need to learn more about business as you embark on the adventure of entrepreneurship or you identify yourself as the creative one and need a counterpart, business can be learned and most often it comes from being self taught.

4. People will think you are weird.

"Entrepreneurs must be willing to be misunderstood for long periods of time." - Jeff Bezos (Amazon)

"When you truly don't care what anyone else thinks of you, you have reached a dangerously awesome level of freedom"
    - Unknown

Marine Corps B.R.A.T.

"Don't get sidetracked by people who are not on track."
- Unknown

Depending on your personality type, being misunderstood may invoke a certain feeling. If you are the individualist type of person this may feel like your happy place. You like (or think you like) being the misunderstood person in a room. The one with the creative, different, maybe even weird, perspective on life. Perhaps this concept of being misunderstood strikes some fear, or insecurity in you. Or possibly you think, "Yes, going against the grain! Against the expected! Stick-it-to-the-man, I'll take being misunderstood!" in a pirate-like, rebel way. However, the key to this comment by Jeff Bezos is "...for long periods of time." It may be fun, rebel-like, or unique to be misunderstood for a little while. Just as long as we can return to our circle of people who *do* understand us when we need a reprieve from all of that being misunderstood. Entrepreneurs may or may not have that safe circle. As an entrepreneur I have learned that even within our own entrepreneur mindset, and even within specific industries it can be difficult to find that circle. A group of people who will champion you and your ideas, who understand what you are after and why, and who want to work as hard and passionately chasing their dreams as you do. Finding a friend or group of people who "get it" can be like trying to catch a leprechaun.

As entrepreneurs we are guaranteed nothing. We spend a lifetime putting ourselves out there, trying things, throwing all our ideas against the wall to see what sticks. Most of the time this is in front of the whole world to see. To let them watch us try and often fail. Leaving us in an emotionally vulnerable position as we chase after what we deem important and worthwhile. It can be draining, exhausting and so, so lonely. Being an entrepreneur, being misunderstood for long periods of time, is not for the faint of heart. However, this does not mean we live lives as hermits, moping about the lack of people who understand our purpose or calling. We were never meant to live in isolation. It is okay to have friends who do not fully understand, who do not comprehend the mission, the passion, the joy of chasing after something. It is okay to be around people who are not fellow entrepreneurs, as long as they are still encouraging and up lifting. Place yourself around positive people, people you want to grow with and do life with. Even though they may not understand your entrepreneurial spirit, they will cheer you on every step of the way. When you have people in your corner you can climb back into the arena, scale the mountain, run the race, fight to the last round, of whatever it is you are after. You will be misunderstood by most, maybe by all, but find people who will encourage you in your bit of madness. This makes the rest of the misunderstanding world tolerable.

5. You may live or you may die by *routine.*

"If you think adventure is dangerous, try routine; it's lethal."
      - Paulo Coelho

Once I had a drivers license and a car the "family meeting" became a nightly routine. There were four of us kids going in different directions everyday of the week. Now that there were three drivers this called for a huddle to determine who was going where, when, and how they would get there. Every day was different growing up. We did not have a rigid schedule and my little Type-A-self thought a daily routine would be a dream come true when I reached adulthood. Soon after I was married I got a glimpse of this and found out it was not my cup of tea. Ironic. Routine, I thought, would give me life and energy, make me feel established and consistent but instead, it unexpectedly drained me. Turns out, I appreciate a morning routine but for the activities of the day to be different each day. When I began writing it was suggested that I establish a "writing space" that is quiet, serene, without distraction, that I go every time I write. This has not worked for me either. Writing takes places at my desk, on the couch, on the floor, at the library, on the deck, wherever I feel so inclined to be that day. Likely, you are questioning how Type-A I really am. There is a piece of me that welcomes flexibility (as long as I am in charge of the flexibility, obviously).

Entrepreneurs understand this. Life is not stagnant or pre-dictable. It is constantly moving like the tide. Ebbing and flowing, in and out, one direction and then the next. Life is alive and happening and routine can sometimes squelch the life out of life. There are people who need routine and I un-derstand that. However, as an entrepreneur, you must to be okay with things changing. With days not being the same. With routines being interrupted. With some messy life being thrown your way. But you are an entrepreneur, you will fig-ure it out.

6. Business will require sacrifice.

"If you don't sacrifice for what you want, what you want becomes the sacrifice." - Unknown

"Whatever you do between 8am and 5pm pays the bills and what you do between 5pm and midnight builds your legacy." - Unknown

As an upper 20 something and a D.I.N.K. (dual-income-no-kids) I often feel like my husband and I ought to be making more money than we are currently. It is easy to compare myself to others in our shoes and wonder how they are paying for their lifestyle. When I get frustrated about where we are financially I quickly jump to the thought, "What if I got a job?" What if I took some of the time I spend working on my businesses and put it towards someone else's business? Someone else's dream? Someone else's passion? Well, when it is put like that it does not make any sense. Why would I do that? To get ahead financially for a moment?

Being a business owner requires sacrifice. Four years ago, I quit a job as a personal trainer to pursue my business full time. It has not been all sunshine and roses, and there are days I wonder if the timing of that decision was right. However, every time I seriously consider getting a job, I remember the sacrifice. Every one of us gets to choose our sacrifice. Are you going to sacrifice the chasing of your dreams or sacrifice the consistent paycheck? By all means make sure you can pay your bills! But take a hard look at what you are sacrificing. Money management expert and radio show host

Dave Ramsey says, "Show me your checkbook and your calendar and I'll show you where your priorities lie." Comedian Steve Harvey recently commented, "Successful people don't sleep eight hours every night, that's a third of your life!" So, where is your sacrifice? Currently, my sacrifice is income. I would rather work at something bigger that will mean more in the long term (by way of impact and income) than sacrifice that work now for a momentary paycheck. Your sacrifice might be overtime, volunteering, social life, or sleep. Take a hard look at your calendar and identify your sacrifice for your business...or where sacrifice needs to be made in order to get where you want to be, because being in business *requires* sacrifice.

7. You *can* be a business owner.

"I can" is 100 times more important than "I.Q."
   - Albert Einstein

Believe. This little component is sorely neglected in almost everything in our daily American lives. It is incredible what simple belief can do in a person. Oh sure, we write "*Believe*" on home decor, charms, and bags etc... thinking we are being inspirational, but then we speak the exact opposite. Simply saying "I can't believe it!" declares in our brains once more that we did not believe something could happen. When going into business for yourself, you have to choose to believe that you can and will make it. This must be a daily practice, a positive attribute you deposit consistently into your mind. Because belief does not just happen, it takes practice. Without belief in your business, in yourself, you will not make it. This basic thought is immensely more important than your I.Q. or your business degree.

"Once you become fearless, life becomes limitless."
     - Unknown

In business fear will always be present in some capacity. There is always something going wrong (and it is likely your fault). The practice of belief combats this mental concern. When you practice belief and understanding, the fear will significantly subside.

"Become best friends with the worst case scenario."
     - Unknown

For years I had this quote on a bulletin board by our front door in one of our homes. Reading it almost daily instilled a subconscious response to fear. Whenever something is going wrong and my brain begins to run wild through every horrible direction this situation could possibly go, this thought slowly seeps in to take over and calm me down. This gives me the freedom to step back from the chaos in my brain, away from all the made up scenarios my thoughts have created, and to think, "What is the very worst, realistic thing that could happen in this situation?" Our imaginations can be amazingly quick causing us to spiral out of control creating ideas and situations that would never actually happen. This thought can bring us back to earth to rationally evaluate the situation and recognize that we can handle (and likely not die from) the very worst case scenario. When you can believe in what you are doing and understand what is going on around you, fear takes a backseat rather than controlling the driver's position. It can be an annoying backseat driver as long as you stay in control. When fear is put in its place you can move forward with clarity and become truly limitless.

"A river cuts through rock, not because of its power, but because of its persistence." - Jim Watkins

Business takes time. It is not a matter of *if* you will be misunderstood, but when, for how long, and by whom? You will work harder than anyone else, agonize over details like no one else, experience heartbreak like no one else, and consider quitting a thousand times. In the end it is the persistent ones, the ones with the most endurance that succeed in business. The ones whose *why* overcomes their fatigue, their mental breakdowns, and their insecurities. The ones who believe that what they are doing matters are the ones who win. So keep going. Continue to press on toward your goal, your dream. Do not give up. Persistence will be the key to your success in business. Practice it, believe in it, and keep going. You *can* be a business owner. You *can* be an entrepreneur.

Keep Growing:
> *How I Built This* podcast
> *Entreleadership* by Dave Ramsey
> *Business Boutique* (book and podcast)
>   by Christy Wright
> *4-Hour Workweek* by Timothy Ferriss

6. Employment

"The only way to do great work is to love what you do."
   - Steve Jobs

"Your profession is not what brings home your paycheck.
Your profession is what you were put on earth to do with
such passion and such intensity that it becomes spiritual in
calling." - Vincent Van Gogh

"Opportunities don't happen, you create them." - Unknown

What if, instead of aptitude tests in your junior year of high
school, you were required to take personality and skills
tests? Perhaps a D.I.S.C., Myers-Briggs or enneagram test.
Possibly, read a book on the subject and then write a report
on your natural strengths and growth areas? How helpful
would that be as you exited school and sought a career path?
Or rather than an advisor instructing that just because you
excel in math you ought to become an engineer, instead they
asked you what types of things interest you and what activities you enjoy? What if classes like shop, cooking, music and
art were not electives. What if you had to give each one a trial run to discover if it could be something you enjoy and
may want to pursue?

My high school boyfriend's aptitude test results suggested he should become a gynecologist. What ridiculous test tells a 17 year old boy he should become a gynecologist?! Another friend had talked of becoming an artist all through high school. He was very skilled and came by it honestly. Meeting up with him a few years into college I learned he had changed his major to teaching because "We will always need teachers." And yet another friend, when analyzing majors in order to select a career path, focused solely on the amount of money he could acquire. Granted, a starting salary of $40,000 sounds exponential to a teenager and when they are all aspiring to be successful millionaires one day. However, the potential income was the primary influence as this friend chose a career.

You may or may not see yourself in one of these scenarios. Perhaps you went to college for a business degree knowing it would provide you a variety of career options. Great! Smart move. Or possibly you are currently sitting in a "safe," "secure" job, with a degree under your belt, and yet, still feeling less than fulfilled. You long to do something you love, something that gives you life, something that makes you feel like you are contributing to the world.
Cue every millennial ever.

The problem is, all too often, we are not encouraged to explore and fail. Failure in itself is a tricky concept. However, exploring is different. What if you had been required to do extensive research on career paths or types of jobs that are options when you have attained a certain degree? What if you had to shadow three different types of careers before you left high school and write a paper on them? Do you think you would still be in the position you are in now? Do you think you would be a little happier? A little more fulfilled?

My dad told us to "Do what you love and the money will come." Specifically, I remember one of these conversations because I could not wrap my head around the theory. My parents made ends meet. We never went hungry and while we were aware of money tension at times it did not negatively affect our childhood. However, I grew up knowing about this tension, seeing, and feeling it. We were not rich (by American standards) and I knew my dad stressed about money. So, when he tells us to do what we love and the money will come, it did not add up. At that point he was driving an hour each way to work a job I knew he hated. This do as I say not as I do stuff was tricky for my half developed teenage brain.

Most teenagers do not struggle to understand this concept because it was never presented to them. Rather than equipping students to understand who they are, identifying their natural skills and interests, and how they can use those to make a career for themselves, we tell them what they are good at based on their school grades. My dad went to school for engineering because he was "good at math." He originally wanted to become a veterinarian. Instead, he has a Bachelor's Degree in Engineering that has never landed him an engineering job. Personally, I have a hard time envisioning him as a vet. However, maybe a better understanding of who he was back then would have saved him a lot of time, frustration, and efforts in the wrong direction. In my mind, I always think of my dad as a Marine. Flying jets in camouflage, in (what I view to be) his natural habitat. It is where he belongs, career-wise (in *my* head at least). He never would have entered the Marine Corps had he not gotten an engineering degree, and then been unable to obtain a job utilizing that degree. Everything tends to work out as it ought to, but the point is that he wanted to be a vet, and nobody encouraged that in him. He was good at math which apparently equals (like it or not) an engineering degree.

Do what you love and the money will come. According to Forbes, 70% of employed adults in the United States are disengaged in their jobs.[10] 70%!! That means 70% feel "less-than" every day in their work. This could have been prevented before leaving school but it was not. Now we have a bunch of unhappy adults who are miserable in their jobs. They go to work only because they have bills due not because their work gives them life and makes them jump out of bed in the morning.

"Here in the city,
We shop in malls,
Eat out in restaurants,
Screen all our calls,
Go to work every mornin'
Behind miles and miles of cars
Just to pay off the interest

---

[10] https://www.forbes.com/sites/davidsturt/2018/03/08/10-shocking-workplace-stats-you-need-to-know/#745bf21f3afe

On our gold MasterCard".
   - *Horse to Mexico* by Triggs Trini

How true are those lyrics?
A. Graduate high school
B. Graduate college so that one day you will "amount to something"
C. Accumulate a mountain of student loans in your journey to "amount to something"
D. Get a job because you must in order to pay the student loans
E. Do all those other things that make you an "adult" (move out, pay bills, get married, have children, move into a bigger space, buy a second car, etc...)
F. Wake up working a job you still do not like but cannot leave because of the bills due. At this point you realize you are one of the 70% of disengaged employees in our country and think, "What happened? How did I get here?"

In my line of work I meet a lot of women. Usually I ask what they do for work in order to engage in conversation and get to know them better. Then I ask, "Do you enjoy it?" About 70% of the time, they hate their jobs. Doing something I love causes me to be even more sympathetic to their situation. They long to be doing something different, something they enjoy that would bring light to their lives and yet they feel stuck.

Prior to getting married I acquired a certification for personal fitness training. Working as a personal trainer, newly married, sharing one vehicle, and striving to make ends meet, I drove home from work one day crying because I was so fed up with my boss' nonsense. Something clicked that day. Driving 30 minutes home from a job I did not love, from a boss I strongly disliked and I was immediately filled with immense appreciation for my dad. For years now he drives an hour each way, to a job he does not enjoy, to pay the bills in order to take care of his family. While I became extremely grateful to him in that moment I also recognized something; that did not have to be me. I did not have a family to provide for (sure, we had nearly no money and were scraping by, but we were doing just that, scraping by). While I appreciated my dad's incredible sacrifice, I recognized that I did not have to sacrifice in the same way. My dad trained us to do what we love and to work for ourselves. Therefore, I was not stuck in my position unless I chose to be. How freeing that thought is!

Did you know this is the same for you? Do you know that we live in the land of the free? That there are immense opportunities all around you? That job offers do not fall out of the sky, but it is incredibly simple to find them online?

My husband, being the sixth of seven children, was the first (and so far, the only) to complete a bachelor's degree.[11] He thought he would go into "ministry" but pursued a business degree in an effort to have more options and so he would

---

[11] *Note: My husband's six siblings simply chose other methods to pursue their selected careers and all are very satisfied where they are today.

better understand how a non-profit business runs. Graduating six months into our marriage he spent a year looking for a job. The business degree gave him too many options. Feeling like a jack-of-all-trades-master-of-none he became very discouraged during this season as he sought a career to pursue. After a long year of job hunting and a friend's referral, he received an offer. The company called us and said, "You can choose California or Rhode Island." Three months later we were packed up, moving away from family and from the second largest U.S. state to the smallest. A state we had never set foot in, a culture we did not expect, but bright-eyed and bushy-tailed heading towards a new adventure in Rhode Island.

After experiencing that year of frustration, I understand that job offers do not fall out of the sky. I also realize that searching for them online, while incredibly easier to find compared to pre-internet days, is not necessarily enjoyable. However, neither is sitting at a job you hate everyday. Paying the bills with a job that you spend at least 67% of your week working does not only pay bills, it affects you and those around you. Have you ever heard someone say, "I will be a better mom when I get some time away?" Or "I am a better person when I take care of myself?" These are not selfish statements, they are true facts! When you are fulfilled and taken care of (by yourself) you can do more for those around you. To offer a money analogy: people who are struggling to pay for their light bill cannot pay for a well to be dug in Africa. In the same way, people who are not taking care of their need for self-actualization, cannot pour themselves out to help or care for others. You are a better friend, spouse, parent, kid, mentor, when you have recognized your personal potential and feel fulfilled. You are better when you are seeking personal growth and peak experiences, when you not only desire, but pursue "becoming everything one is capable of becoming."[12]

If this is not the way it has to be, if you are not literally "stuck" in your position, how do you change it?

1. Growth vs. Victim Mentality

Decide to not be stuck.

You have to make the decision yourself. If you are working a job you hate, providing for a family and/or specific lifestyle, it is incredibly easy to be convinced that you cannot move or change the situation. "We must have this income," or "We cannot move the family," or "This job is the right distance from our home," are all excuses I have heard from *stuck* people. Most of whom never sought out their options, but instead, owned their current situation as truth and sat in it indefinitely.

Carol Dweck, a psychologist at Stanford University, established the concept of a growth vs. a fixed mentality. This idea tackles the way we view others and what we believe about ourselves. Those with a "growth mindset" believe that their intelligence can be further developed, they welcome challenges, and see failure as a learning tool not a death sen-

---

[12] Maslow, 1987, p.64 https://www.simplypsychology.org/maslow.html

tence. On the other hand, those with a "fixed mindset" or "victim mentality" believe that character, intelligence, and creative ability are static features inherited at birth. If static, why pursue more or challenge anything?[13]

When you begin looking for it, you will quickly recognize these two types of people and their mindsets in your own life. Listen to the way people speak. Do they speak looking for solutions or complaining about where they are? Those who claim they have no options, this is it, right here, the best it is going to get; those are victim thinkers. Steer clear if you want to live a life of opportunity and positivity.

Which one are you currently? If you are struggling realizing you have a victim mentality or "fixed mindset," chin up! Turns out you do not have to stay in that mindset! You have the power to adjust and change your life in the process.

Our mindset will positively or negatively affect every area of our lives. It will also affect your job and career. The first step to getting "unstuck" is to decide you are not stuck. Once you realize that you have options, that you do not have to stay where you are, freedom and opportunities are yours for the taking. Dave Ramsey says, "The one with the most options wins." Do not be a loser by giving yourself only one option. Find more options. Do not be a victim and convince yourself

---

[13] https://www.brainpickings.org/2014/01/29/carol-dweck-mindset/
https://www.developgoodhabits.com/fixed-mindset-vs-growth-mindset/

there are no other options. There are always more options. Go find the options. Move. You are not a tree.

2. Explore Yourself

Early in our dating relationship my husband introduced me to the D.I.S.C. personality test. He had taken the test during a leadership program at church, found it fascinating, and wanted to see my results. He quickly briefed me on what each letter meant, I took the test, and then I cried. At the time, Josh was a C and I scored as a C as well. Somehow, in his quick explanation of everything, I came to understand that two people of the same personality could never make a romantic relationship work. Therefore, I cried. I was under the impression that we could never get married. Upset and frustrated, I thought we may as well call this whole thing quits. He had to bend over backwards to re-explain the concept of the test. I was still skeptical for awhile, but I came around and well…it *can* work.

This began my exploration of who I was. That year was formative for me in understanding my personal habits; what was important to me, what my personality was and what I wanted out of life. Most people do not take time to answer these questions for themselves. Taking a test to discover your letter on the D.I.S.C. or your number on the Enneagram is fine, but ultimately useless unless you also take time to understand what the results mean. In turn, when you learn about yourself, you also learn about others around you.

Understanding more about yourself can help you discover what Ken Coleman calls your "sweet spot." The place where who you are, your natural abilities, and what you love, collide to create your true dream job. A highly personable, energetic, idea-a-minute kind of person should probably not be in accounting. They would likely enjoy life more in marketing. Shy, soft-spoken, introverted, go-with-the-flow should not be a car salesman. CPA or IT would likely be a better fit. Obviously, these are generalizations. Unfortunately, all too often these basic concepts are not considered when selecting a degree, job or career path.[14]

Take some time to learn who you are. Here is a list of personality tests, most of which can be found for free online. The key to taking these tests is to not overthink your answers. Answer the questions with your gut reaction. Then, identify what it means to be your personality type.

- D.I.S.C.
- Enneagram
- Myers-Briggs

---

[14] *Note: finding your sweet spot, your dream job does not necessarily equate to discovering your "passion." There is too much buzz around the word "passion," specifically amidst my millennial generation. The problem with finding your passion is that passions change. They are fleeting. As soon as you "find your passion" it may fly away into something else and you are left empty-handed still seeking. Please do not get caught up in finding your "passion." Instead, discover what means the most to you, what your skills and interests are, and build your life and career from there.

- Birth Order Theory
- 4 Temperaments
- 5 Love Languages

In addition to learning your natural personality and temperament, explore what you enjoy. What would you do every day, all day if you could? What would you do for free because you love it so much? Make a list! Then, analyze your list a bit…if you love basketball but you are four-foot-nothing we can safely cross off "NBA superstar" from your potential career list. However, do not cross off the fact that basketball is something that you love. Simply mark which things combine what you are good at and also love.

Your "sweet spot" should be coming to light during this self-exploration. Who are you? What is your personality like? What are you naturally good at? What do you love to do? What do you wish you could get paid to do because it would feel like you were not working?

3. Explore the Possibilities

My mom tells a story about a friend of hers who added "fishing" to the "hobbies" or "things I enjoy" portion of his résumé. He figured, "What could it hurt?" That man got a job fishing. Not just fishing to fish, he collects water samples and studies the fish for the Smithsonian in the Chesapeake Bay. He was able to work in a lucrative position and he got to do his very favorite activity all day, every day.

Moral of the story: *Definitely* put your hobbies on your résumé.
Moral of the story part two: There are always more options. Find them.

The year my husband spent looking for a job just out of college was rough on him. He felt like a jack-of-all-trades-master-of-none. Decent at everything he put his hands to but not outstanding or passionate about anything. This made it extremely hard to seek out jobs after attaining a business degree that almost anyone will accept. He is introverted, hardworking, consistent, system-driven, even-keeled, and logical. For six years he has been working in sales. Upon graduating college he did not think he would love to get a job in sales, but it is a great job that he enjoys.

There are always more options.

Obtaining a degree in nursing does not mean you must become a nurse. There are more positions in which you can utilize your degree and not necessarily work in a hospital or doctor's office. A family friend who was once an interior designer went back to school for teaching. She spent several years in the classroom only to hate it and now she teaches special education students online from her home and loves her job.

What is your sweet spot? Where do your natural abilities, skills, interests, and passions meet up? What jobs are out there in that realm? Go exploring. Find absurd positions you never knew existed!

My husband and I had no idea there were people out there working something called "inside service sales" on industrial sized computer back-ups. But there were and he became one of them.

4. A Degree Does Not Make You A _____

You might be taking in all this information and thinking, "All of this would have been great to know in high school, or college, or before I got myself 15 years into a career." Where you are right now dictates *nothing* about your future unless you choose to let life happen to you. If you went to school for something specific (nurse, engineer, teacher, etc…) and you are not fulfilled or it is not what you thought it would be, you are not stuck there. A degree in a specific field does not mean you must spend the rest of your life in that field. However, there are likely other options within your field you do not know about. Seek them out. Nonetheless, if you feel a pull in a completely new direction, do not shut it down. Do not deny that thought. Do not ignore it, or push it from your mind because of what others have told you. Do not believe the lies that your current situation will not allow for a new direction.

Too often, we have been led to believe that a college degree equals experience and a career. I absolutely want my doctor to have a degree. Although, I also do not want to be the first person he diagnoses or cuts open. Doctors need to have experience in their field. As for the guy who does my taxes, as long as he knows his stuff I do not care what school he attended or how many letters come before or after his name. Just do my taxes correctly. To become a personal trainer I acquired a certification online through a self-paced program. At my first job my co-worker had a degree in kinesiology from Michigan State University. She also had two additional certifications more prestigious than mine. Yet, we were both making the same amount per client at this job.

Not all jobs require a degree. Do not dare think that going in a different direction will first require years of schooling. Do the exploring, find out what that direction will require. Can you pass the bar exam without taking two years of prerequisites (that have nothing to do with law or passing the bar)? Can you get yourself around others in that field to find out what their day-to-day looks like? What tasks and knowledge does the job really require? Push the envelope a little bit, challenge the societal standard that everyone needs a degree in order to do anything. What can you do without one?[15]

5. Pursue Without Limits

Have you discovered your sweet spot? Did you find a list of jobs you never knew existed in your field?

Get after it! Whether it is a specific job, position or company. Go after it! Do not let anything inhibit you.

During that year of job searching for my husband, his brother in California continued to encourage us, "Don't just look

[15] *Refer to the list in the previous chapter for people in different industries that have succeeded without a college degree.

for jobs in Texas! You guys are young and free and the world is at your fingertips! Look for jobs everywhere!" As simple as that sounds, it opened our eyes and minds. Who was to say we could not or should not move to North Carolina, Washington, or Australia? Why not? We had nothing to lose! And you do not either. My generation is obsessed with living close to family. My family is the best in the world. My three siblings are some of my very best friends. Yet, we moved away. I am a Marine Corps brat…moving is what we do, right? While family will always be thick as blood, the best jobs and opportunities for a fulfilled life are not always in close proximity to them. And that is okay. You will miss them like crazy and wish you could stop by their place just to say hi. You may long for a last minute babysitter or to assist them with the spring yard work, but you will survive all these things.

Do not let your geographical location limit you. You are limitless. The world is at your fingertips. You are not stuck. You can go anywhere and be anything you long to be. Get after it!

The house will sell, you will find a new one. The kids will adjust and find new friends. There are more churches, community groups and great neighbors in other towns. Where you live is not perfect and the next place will not be either. And that is okay. Give yourself permission to experience different places.

Six years ago my husband found a job, after a year of searching, that moved us to a state we had never stepped foot in. It was scary and adventurous. Today, we love our little state and this region. We cannot imagine never having experienced this beautiful place. You never know what you could experience when you get out of your box. Step out of your comfort zone. Give yourself some options. Explore this great, big, beautiful world that we live in. Live without limits.

A note on money: if you *feel* stuck because of financial commitments I highly recommend taking the course *Financial Peace University* by Dave Ramsey. Go to his website to find the class nearest to you. When you experience life without debt and make a plan for your money, you will be amazed at the freedoms and opportunities it opens up to you. Before committing time to writing this book I felt the need to contribute more to our income and began looking for a part-time job. After talking it over with Josh he said to me, "Unless that part-time job is something you want to be doing, don't do it. I would rather you put your time and effort into something you want to pursue, like writing your book. We do not have any debt and we are living well beneath our means. You do not have to get another job." The freedom in that statement brought me to tears. He was absolutely right. When you are free from debt and live below your means it gives you margin in your money and time to pursue the things you love and long for. I want you to experience that same kind of freedom, within your money, your time, and your career.

Move. You are not a tree.

Keep Growing:

The Proximity Principle by Ken Coleman
Roadmap by Roadtrip Nation
The Ken Coleman Show Podcast
financialpeace.com
ianmorgancron.com/assessment

7. Independence

"The first of earthly blessings, independence."
   - Edward Gibbon

"Those that can give up essential liberty to gain a little temporary safety deserve neither liberty nor safety."
   - Benjamin Franklin

"May we think of freedom, not as the right to do as we please, but as the opportunity to do what is right."
   - Peter Marshall

What do you think of when you hear the word "independence?" An image of those majestic stars and stripes flapping in the wind? Do stories of heroes and bravery trickle through your mind? Or maybe you think of demanding toddlers or feisty teenagers. What feeling does this word stir up inside of you? Is it pride? Gratitude? Intimidation? Fear?

Two things come to mind for me: the Revolutionary War and teenagers.

"Let the American youth never forget, that they possess a noble inheritance, bought by the toils, and sufferings, and blood of their ancestors; and capacity, if wisely improved, and faithfully guarded, of transmitting to their latest pos-

terity all the substantial blessings of life, the peaceful enjoyment of liberty, property, religion, and independence."
- *Commentaries on the Constitution* by Joseph Story (1833)

The Revolutionary War began in April of 1775. In 1778, three years into the war, we brought in an experienced German military man, Baron Friedrich Wilhelm von Steuben, to help us train our weary and novice troops. He arrived just after the long, punishing winter at Valley Forge to restore morale, instill discipline and coherence, and whip the soldiers into fighting shape. Baron von Steuben was respected and much needed for his military experience. Within two weeks, George Washington made him acting inspector general. While respected by the men under him, this distinguished, veteran and military officer quickly realized he was dealing with a different kind of army.

"And though the baron was appalled at the condition of the army he was tasked with making over, he soon developed an appreciation for its soldiers. "The genius of this nation is not in the least to be compared with that of the Prussian, Austrians, or French," von Steuben wrote to a Prussian friend. "You say to your soldier 'Do this and he doeth it'; but I am obliged to say [to the American soldier]: 'This is the reason why you ought to do that: and then he does it.'"
- *The Prussian Nobleman Who Helped Save the American Revolution* by Erick Trickey[16]

---

[16] https://www.smithsonianmag.com/history/baron-von-steuben-180963048/

Marine Corps B.R.A.T.

"They said all
Teenagers scare
The living shit out of me
They could care less
As long as someone'll bleed
So darken your clothes
Or strike a violent pose
Maybe they'll leave you alone
But not me"
       - *Teenagers* by My Chemical Romance

My Chemical Romance hit the nail on the head. Anyone else slightly scared of teenagers?

Like any word, context has the power to induce different feelings or emotions. Perhaps you have never considered this. Independence may be scary to you or something you think is not for you and your personality, when in reality, it has always been inside of you. You have the power and responsibility to be independent.

> "What we obtain too cheap, we esteem too lightly: it is dearness only that gives every thing its value. Heaven knows how to put a proper price upon its goods; and it would be strange indeed if so celestial an article as freedom should not be highly rated." - Thomas Paine

There are two problems with this word in our current society. First, we need both independence and dependence. We were not created to live this life alone pushing relationships away from us. Toddlers know where their food comes from but get quickly mixed up when they want their way and also want food. They lack comprehension of how to balance these desires and relationships. The second problem is how some are generally, possibly even subconsciously, taught to feel towards this word or concept. We are blessed with so much at our fingertips in this country that we have learned to rely on others too heavily. Rather than grasping a heavy dose of independence, by taking care of ourselves, we tend to shy away. Leaving much of what happens to us up to other people. There has been fear instilled in us towards this concept, that independence is somehow risky, scary, or even unlikable in a person. In turn, this has formed a perspective that independence is bad, excessive or unnecessary. As though the one who takes everything about their life into their own hands is trying too hard, pushing limits, or being over the top. Consider a boy who so badly desires to be viewed as a man that he goes over the top to be macho. No one likes that guy trying desperately to be a man's man. It is a similar distaste that people project on those who are fiercely independent.

Independence is something we are born with. Independence is not only for the brave and courageous. Independence is coursing through our veins. We tend to notice it more in teenagers because they have more freedoms than when they were young children. Parenting is a balancing act of loosening the leash and guiding their choices as they explore and learn the newfound freedoms of adulthood. Independence is a biological part of who we are and is necessary to live a happy and thriving life.

Marine Corps B.R.A.T.

"Independence is happiness" - Susan B. Anthony

Consider infancy when babies are 100% reliant on their parents for survival. Not only for attachment and love but bare-bones survival. Upon reaching toddler stage the independence in our blood begins to rear its head and drive parents crazy. There is madness in trying to understand a demanding small human who cannot yet tell you what they want! Through childhood we see the back and forth, the challenge in finding balance between independence and dependence. Children rely on their parents for guidance, discipline, safety, housing, clothing, food, love etc... And yet, they want freedom to make some choices themselves. We see this played out when a frazzled parent shows up with a child wearing polka dots paired with stripes. Mom lost the battle that day or decided it was not worth fighting. Prior to adolescence, children seek the approval of their parents above any other person. As adolescence approaches, they begin to value the approval of their peers over their parents. This causes a stronger desire for more independence while still needing the care, guidance, and provision of their parents, simultaneously, their heart tugs them toward peer approval.

There appears to be a mutual understanding that teenagers rebel. That all teenagers dislike their parents, disagree with them, believe that they know better, and want to do their own thing. Unfortunately, adolescent years are a tough place to navigate. Not many people would willingly relive those years. Whoever said high school should be the best four years of life was on drugs. Or living a pitiful, discouraging adult life. My understanding of adulthood and parenting (thus far) is that it is all a crapshoot. Everyone is faking it and trying to make it by with a smile on our faces. The thing about teenagers (besides puberty and raging hormones) is that they are approaching adulthood but they are not there yet. Adolescence is just like any other strange in-between season to navigate.

My husband and I dated for nine months and were engaged for 10 months. I firmly believe that engagement is the worst part of a relationship. There are certainly difficult parts about dating and marriage, but engagement is the worst and I highly recommend keeping that season as brief as possible. Two people have decided to commit their lives to each other but there is a culturally understood season of waiting before they can actually begin that life together. Get great pre-marital counseling in that season, by all means, but it does not have to take months or years to do this or to plan a wedding. Get on with the life and marriage part after the wedding.

Buying a house is another similar situation. There is a terrible in-between stage like engagement when purchasing a home. We have signed the documents, the seller has signed documents, a realtor, a mortgage broker, a lender, a painter, a floor refinisher, inspector, and an appraiser all want to move forward and get the process completed but everybody is waiting on somebody. Usually this waiting is 45-60 days. Not quite as long as most American engagements but it is still an in-between waiting period that is less than enjoyable.

Thus is adolescence. This is being a teenager. Your brain is mostly developed, you have been given some freedoms and you are chomping at the bit to try out your newly acquired wings, but you are not allowed to do so just yet. You have authority figures everywhere attempting to mold you, guide you and hold you back, to make you think about your choices and it is exhausting. You just want to leave the house without telling anyone where you are going or what you are doing. The desire for independence eats away at the hearts of teenagers and usually manifests itself as rebellion. Likely, most teenagers do not intend to be rebellious, most do not hate their parents or even disagree with them, they only want the opportunity to make their own choices.

Independent is defined as:
1. Not influenced or controlled by others in matters of opinion, conduct, etc.; thinking for and acting for oneself.
2. Not subject to another's authority or jurisdiction; autonomous; free.
3. Not influenced by the thought or action of others.
4. Not dependent; not depending or contingent upon something else for existence, operation, etc.
5. Freedom from the control, influence, support, aid, or the like, of others.   (dictionary.com)

Unfortunately, like most things in life, there must be balance in independence. Too much and you become a loner or like that macho guy that nobody likes. Someone reminded me once that a scale (the old-timey kind with plates on either end that even out with each oth-er and were used to measure) is never stagnant. The scale is ever moving, ever balancing. Its job of weighing, of balancing, never ends. We get caught up in seeking the key, the one trick, the solution to "balance" in our lives, when the truth is, there is no such thing. Balance will never be achieved. However, we can achieve harmony if we properly pursue it.

Harmony means there is give and take in different seasons. Let's view this from a time standpoint: everyone is trying to figure out how to "balance" their schedule and time. Harmony within time means that some days some areas of life need more attention than other areas. Sometimes your kids are more needy or you are in the middle of a big project or focused on a goal for a short season. It is alright to ebb and flow. Not every area of life will receive the same amount of time every day. In the same way, we can seek harmony in our lives between being independent and dependent on others.

A marriage of two totally independent people will not last, in order to work together they have to depend on one another. Often, I tease my husband that if he were to die suddenly there would be a list of things I would be clueless on how to do around our home. For example, I have never strung lights on a Christmas tree, he knows the correct ratio of gin to tonic, I am forever baffled by how bluetooth works, the thermostat would never get moved down, the blinds never adjusted, and the pictures on my phone would be gone forever. I would be lost without him! Obviously, these things would not be the end of me were the good Lord to take my sweet husband. However, it is an example of how I rely on him. As independent and "Don't tell me what to do!" as I am, I need him and others in my life in many ways. Independence is lonely without balance, and while born with independence in us, we were not made to be alone either.

"Freedom is only part of the story and half the truth…That is why I recommend that the Statue of Liberty on the East Coast be supplanted by a Statue of Responsibility on the West Coast." - *Man's Search for Meaning* by Viktor E. Frankl

"If ye love wealth better than liberty, the tranquility of servitude better than the animating contest of freedom, go home from us in peace. We ask not your counsels or your arms. Crouch down and lick the hands which feed you. May your chains set lightly upon you, and may posterity forget that you were our countrymen." - Samuel Adams

There is a difference between independence and freedom, they are not one and the same. If they were the same, they would not have been paired together twice in the Declaration of Independence. Twice it says we are to be "Free and

Independent States." While freedom is the ability to be free from the control of others, independence is taking advantage of that freedom. Freedom is the power to do and decide. It is personal liberty. However, independence is freedom in action. It is the responsibility to do something with the freedoms rendered to you. Independence is not only not being under the control of someone else's commands, but being completely free of their influence, opinion, or conduct. While each of us is granted freedoms in the United States of America it is independence that takes hold of that freedom and wields its power. Without independence, freedom is useless. What good is the freedom of free speech or the freedom to bear arms if we are too far under the influence, opinion or conduct of others to speak freely or own a gun? If you are not going to uphold and take care of these freedoms, why bother living in the home of the free? There are plenty of other countries where you would fit in better if you dislike the freedoms offered here. Independence is taking hold of freedoms granted to us. Just as we covered taking control of your time and your future in entrepreneurial ventures, independence is claiming control of your thoughts, and your actions without the influence of others.

Freedom and independence are longed for, fought for and praised and have been since the dawn of time. America was not the first in the world's history to fight for our freedom. However, it is one of the most epic stories of determination and fighting for one's values: freedom and independence.

America was discovered, settlers came to the new land, some for the promise of wealth and adventure but most for the sake of religious *freedom*. Hoping to be outside the long arm of the law of an oppressing monarch. For over 200 years the people in this far off land were still controlled by royalty who lived across an ocean. This was not the freedom they had bargained for. Finally, the inhabitants of our 13 colonies had enough. They banded together and mustered up the courage to fight against anyone who threatened their freedom and independence. With generations of pent up anger, the Americans questioned everything. Returning to Baron von Steuben, rather than simply obeying orders the soldiers needed to know the *why* behind the commands. Overall, and to this day, in military, this is extremely dangerous. Usually, an authority figure has been put in a place of authority for a reason, with a purpose, and experience. They have every right and responsibility to tell you what to do, and Lord knows you better do it, or lives (possibly yours) could be on the line. You may not see the reason for the instruction or how it matters. But it does. During basic training in military branches today they work hard to beat this into (or out of...?) new recruits. Basic training is created to be extremely difficult because they have to retrain, rewire, and reeducate the new recruits. The weak disqualify themselves. The hardheaded either come to their own demise or learn the lessons and rise to the top. However, the lesson learned in these trainings is to not question authority, but to obey and do so immediately. It may mean life or death.

This independence thing was an "issue" from our country's beginning. It has been running through our American veins since our country began. These people had been told how to live their lives by a monarch far too long and they were sick and tired of it. We were not to be pushed around by a king across an ocean, an army sent by him, or even by a general attempting to help us win the fight. Because of their fight so long ago, because of their questioning, their pent up anger, and their courage, we have freedoms today that much of the world is not privileged to claim. While we relish in this privilege, are we taking full advantage of it? While we attempt to balance the scales of independence and dependence on others, are we slowly losing ground in our independence?

You must have an ebb and flow of independence and dependence on others for a healthy and thriving life. The problem is what our current culture does not teach us about independence. Unfortunately, much of our education system has caused people to learn to be dependent on a system. Radio personality and author, Ken Coleman, says our school system has created a culture of "test takers rather than path finders." He means that our students are trained to ace tests and not to actually learn or find new ways to explore or fail. "Get good grades, go to college, so you can get a good job," the simple phrase that so many have had drilled into their heads is about dependence on this system. "Pass the test and move forward," sounds like dependence on a system more than independence, and even neglects basic self-sufficiency.

"Get good grades" - while this ought to rely on your studying, learning capabilities and discipline, oftentimes it is subject to the teacher. You are dependent on the teacher for your grades and learning. We are not taught to learn on our own.

"Go to college" - another place where we rely on others to inform us if we are learning well enough. Except that now the stakes are higher because we have been told these grades will affect our job and financial status for the rest of our lives.

"Get a good job" - so that you can rely completely on someone else issuing you the money that provides for your lifestyle. Where you are dependent on someone else for your complete livelihood with no control over what happens. I sense no danger here (*sarcasm*).

Unfortunately it seems this system that we are required to follow for the first two decades of our life, has accidentally wiped the independence out of us. Nearly 20% of men and 12% of women, age 25-34, were living in their parent's homes in 2017 according to an article published by washingtonpost.com. One may argue this is due to surmounting college debts, lack of jobs and/or increased living expenses. However, it is my concern that it is due to a lack of independence. Were these young people not able to establish themselves as independent adults or were they fearful of doing so? For so long they had others to rely on. Is it that they may never have been given the space to learn how to separate themselves from the nest? To survive and thrive as independent adults?

While poor Baron von Steuben was perplexed, and likely frustrated, by our American need to challenge everything, he also admired it. That push back, the independence by nature is what won that war and every war since. That independence is what fires us up when we are under attack. Don't mess with us not only because we are Americans, but because we live in freedom and we are never relinquishing that!

> "A strong body makes the mind strong. As to the species of exercises, I advise the gun. While this gives moderate exercise to the body, it gives boldness, enterprise and independence to the mind. Games played with the ball, and others of that nature, are too violent for the body and stamp no character on the mind. Let your gun therefore be your constant companion of your walks."
> - Thomas Jefferson

Returning to early in our country's beginnings one last time, the people who founded our country were incredible! They were ruthless! Can you imagine hopping on a boat and traveling to an unknown land only to arrive and have to build your own house and form your own government? All for the sake of freedom and independence? How about loading the family into a covered wagon to head west into uncharted territory in hopes of owning some property. Again, only to get there and have to construct your own home and sleep under the stars until it was complete? There is bravery and courage galore in story after story about our country's beginning. However, what I want to point out here is what they were teaching their kids. If you read these stories those people were not very different from us. They were young and determined to make the best life possible for themselves. They went after what they wanted and were unsure and terrified every step of the way. However, they were given loads of responsibility at younger ages and the expectations set for them were astronomical compared to what we expect from kids (or even ourselves) today. These people did not have the option to rely on others for much of what we do today. They certainly needed community and family for acceptance and support, needs we all inherently have. However, many did not have the option to rely on lawmakers, peacekeepers, judges, doctors or teachers. If their kids were going to learn to read it was up to parents to teach them. With no formal system for keeping the peace, they could not call 9-1-1 in an emergency, but taught their children and families to defend themselves. In one sense, it is incredibly convenient to have others to rely on for these things today. However, complete dependence on them renders you vulnerable to the teachings or to the systems in place. Complete dependence on others makes you prey to others while independence gives you power to not be the victim. Nobody attacks the lion, the king of the jungle.

"You don't tug on Superman's cape.
You don't spit into the wind.
You don't pull the mask off that old Lone Ranger.
And you don't mess around with Jim."
...or something like that (thanks Jim Croce).

We are born juggling this scale of independence vs dependence, but do not think that grabbing hold of independence will be easy. Just because we have independence built into our make-up does not mean coaxing it out will be effortless. And that is okay. Most things worth doing are not easy. Embrace the difficult and know that moving forward will be worth every bit of hard.

It goes without saying, do not be a bully. That is not what independence is about. Independence is about handling your own stuff, taking care of business, protecting and defending yourself, "adulting" if you will. We must balance independence and dependence. However, from where I stand, most in our culture today could use a gallon more independence in them than what they have right now. So, I challenge you, where are you being independent in your life right now? Where could you take hold of more independence in your life? What area can you claim more responsibility for?

One way to find this area in your life is to ask yourself, "Where do I feel like a victim?" Do you feel defenseless against someone stronger than you? Take a self-defense class. Do you feel like you do not have the edge up on the competition? What could you read or do to teach yourself to give you that one-up? Do you feel like a rat caught in the wheel of life? What change can you make to get out of the rat race? Where do you fall victim and what can you do to take responsibility for your independence by doing something to change that? If you are a college graduate living with your parents I hope not to shame you, but to put a fire under your belly to grow up. Whether it is moving out, paying your own bills, waking yourself up in the morning, or recognizing nobody is going to hand you your dream job. Whoever you are, go out there and take hold of your independence.

"Independence .... is loyalty to one's best self and principles, and this is often disloyalty to the general idols and fetishes."
- Mark Twain

Keep Growing:
> *The Road to Freedom* by Arthur C. Brooks
> *How An Economy Grows and Why It Crashes*
> by Peter D. Schiff

8. Community

"Practice of true community involves responsibilities and actions that do not come naturally to us." - Jerry Bridges

"We are created for community, fashioned for fellowship, and formed for a family, and none of us can fulfill God's purposes by ourselves." - Rick Warren

"Saying yes feels good, but a great relationship is one where you can say no and everyone is totally ok with it."
   - Dr. Henry Cloud

When I was in seventh grade, my family moved from a temporary townhouse in Virginia to a 50 acre camp in Pennsylvania. At this time, I had maneuvered the entirety of sixth grade in a season of transition as my family moved several times. In many ways the season of transition was tolerable. However, it was greatly lacking in the friendship department. Melodramatic and "martyr-esque," I resolved to survive without friends and eventually renew my search for these relationships when in college (cue a sad, longing look out a somber, paned glass window). While my parents had always involved us in activities and sports for access to friendships, this had been a funky 18 months of no-man's-land. Two days after my commitment to teenage solitude a neighbor invited me to her son's youth group. Once again, I was immersed in friendships that carried me through middle and high school. Hope was restored to my 13 year old soul.

Within six months of moving to a new state (and only 18 months into our marriage) my husband and I had more friends than we could keep up with. We had planted ourselves into a church home group with couples our age. We had taken every opportunity to get together, grab coffee or lunch, and quickly found ourselves with quality relationships. A year later my parents came to visit and participated in our latest home group which met in our apartment. After everyone left, my dad opened a beer, and they poured on some wisdom. My parents reminisced about their first real community as a married couple. Stationed in Florida, shortly after being married, they found a church and group of friends to "do life with" before that phrase existed. They warned us to soak up these moments. That this season will likely be short. Wonderful as it is, it will end, and you may never achieve that level of community again. Six months later three of our closest couple friends informed us of impending moves across the country and our little group was disbanded. My parents were not wrong.

Maybe you have had friends and lost them. Possibly you have never experienced real depth in friendships, the kind you imagine others possess. Perhaps you feel lonely, or bogged down by your friends. It may be, you have too many friends. Maybe one of these is you and you are wondering what to do with this community piece of your life.

Friendship is a finicky relationship. It is unpredictable, ever-changing, evolving, and it is optional. We long for it, yet we are often not equipped to manage and cultivate it. Not all families are like my own. However, as a generalized statement, families are forever. Families stick together. They take care of one another, love on each other etc. Those relationships are intended to be a lifelong support system. For most of us, we know how to manage and maintain our families. We were groomed to be part of a family unit. Friendships on the other hand, are tricky. Friends can shift in and out of our lives. Friends can be acquaintances, co-workers, drinking buddies, kindred spirits. You can choose to invite them into your life and also escort them out. Even the dictionary includes an array of options for what a friend is:

1. A person attached to another by feelings of affection or personal regard
2. A person who gives assistance; patron; supporter
3. A person who is on good terms with another; a person who is not hostile
4. A member of the same nation, party, etc.
 (dictionary.com)

Likely, you have someone you would call a friend in each of these categories. In fact, we call all 876 of the people we are connected with on Facebook our "friends" while only mildly connected to many of them. What is friendship sincerely all about? Is it worth opening ourselves, becoming vulnerable, engaging in life with people even if it might be for only a short while?

Luckily, it does not have to be so complex! Did you know there are guidelines to handling people and friendships? Family is incredibly important to our lives, but they have to be handled with care. No one reading this book can say they have never experienced a family crisis, hiccup, or dispute. If you cannot say the same about your friendships, it may be time to reevaluate what you call a friend. Even though these relationships are tricky, and evolve, change or may come and go, they can be navigated with grace and balance. This need in our life can be satisfying and fulfilling without being a burden. These relationships can be a joy and bring even more life and love to your existence.

1. Why community?

We were made for this.

Proverbs 27:10 (ESV)
"Do not forsake your friend and your father's friend, and do not go to your brother's house in the day of your calamity. Better is a neighbor who is near than a brother who is far away."

Many friends have come and gone in my lifetime. However, my immediate family (my parents and three siblings) have always been present through thick and thin, every trial, every success, and countless inside jokes. My very best friends are within my family unit. There is a unique connection when you have people in your life for your entire life. People who understand everything about how you were raised and were present for every experience. However,

134

Marine Corps B.R.A.T.

"Better is a neighbor who is near than a brother who is far away."

A two hour drive, briefly in my teen years, was the the closest we ever lived to family. Being military, we learned that community, friends, become your local family. We attempted to spend holidays with blood relatives, but with four kids and living across the country that was not always feasible. We spent many a Thanksgiving and Easter with dear, local friends.

Why community? Because we are not made to be alone. The fact that we are born into families, born of two people who are (supposed) to play the roles of two parents thus, creating a small community immediately upon birth, shows us this. While this "ideal" situation is not always reality, it shows us we were not made to be isolated. Sometimes we have to manufacture our family, but we always have to construct our community. In addition to that the Bible references the word "friend" 111 times. Many of these references are "go to your friends" as if they are always gathered and waiting for whoever is receiving this instruction.

As newlyweds we lived in Dallas, Texas so my husband could finish his undergraduate degree. We lived within 30 minutes of my husband's parents and three of his siblings. While these people are dear to us, we sought to establish separate friendships. Not to stake our territory, "Ah-ha! See, we are adults and this is our arena!" but to establish some relationships and community of our own. Learning to do this early gave us the skills we needed to build community when we moved to a new state where we did not know a soul. Community in a foreign place is absolutely necessary. The popular phrase the kids are using today is "do life with." We need people physically around us for the good and the bad times. Someone who brings you a meal, picks you up at the airport, swings by with ice cream when you are feeling down. People who help you pack and clean your home when you have to fly out of town on a moment's notice for a family funeral. When you do not have family nearby, you need people in your life to take on that role. Introvert or extrovert, we cannot go through this life alone. We need community.

2. What is community?

"It takes a village to raise a child." - African proverb

How many people are in the average child's life? Teachers, daycare workers, doctors, parents, neighbors, pastors, etc. everyone working to guide the child. This is community, and we do not relinquish the need for it when we turn 18. Whether navigating tough seasons of life, or enjoying successes, community is present for you in the good and bad.

Community should be more than peers. My mom used to get frustrated about this in public schools. She would say, "The only time in life you will be completely surrounded by only people your age is in school." The claim is that this format sets children up for success when really, it often handicaps them, preventing them from understanding how to communicate with people outside their own age group.

Community involves variety. We need peers who are in a similar chapter of life. However, we also need older and wiser people who can help us navigate through life gracefully, people who have been through it all before us. In addition, it is our duty to be those older, and hopefully wiser, people to others. Community is built of all ages assisting each other through life, because there is not a guide for each chapter.

A specific sermon that impacted me years ago came from a youth pastor I briefly worked alongside. He shared a story of recently having dental work done. In Maryland, a tornado threat is a rare occurrence. However, on that particular day a tornado was headed that way and this guy was attempting to play the role of protecting husband and dad to four small kids and a puppy while on dental drugs. Staggering about the house, trying to get his brain to think clearly, wrangle up the family and figure out what to do with them he thought, "There is no chapter in a guidebook titled "What to do when drugged during a tornado threat when you have four small children." This example has come to mind many times in my life. There is no guidebook. There is no chapter on "How to properly comfort your introverted husband after his dad dies" or "Next steps after your car catches on fire" or "When you have dropped the only car key into a water drain do this." This is why we need community, and why we need variety in that community. While no one may have experienced your *exact* situation, "Two heads are better than one." Having more people of different ages, stages, and walks of life in your corner gives you the best chance for success in navigating this crazy life.

Proverbs 27:9 (ESV)
"Oil and perfume make the heart glad, and the sweetness of a friend comes from his earnest counsel."

3. How do we "*community*?"

The first thing to do after a move to a new place is find a "home church." Of course, this can only be pursued on Sundays. Therefore, every week you go "church shopping." It is a tedious and frustrating process. The key to finding the right church for your family is to seek one that believes in the Bible, acts on those beliefs, and has a strong sense of community. As a newcomer to a church, city or state, you want to feel like you belong, to feel a little less like a foreigner. When my husband and I moved to Rhode Island we only tried out three churches (rather than the 12 we tried in Texas). At the third church, a woman introduced herself to us. After service she spoke with us more and invited us to a meet-and-greet after the service. At the meet-and-greet we met several more people who were genuinely interested in us and the rest is history. This church hooked us because of how we were treated. These people expressed genuine care and interest in who we were instead of a flippant, dutiful hello and returning to their own friends.

Finding a church quickly after a new move is really a search for community. Community and friendships do not fall into your lap. They must be pursued, sought after, engaged, and maintained. These are relationships, and every relationship takes some level of work. However, these specific relationships, friendships, can be tricky to maneuver when you have never received guidelines on how to properly manage and maintain them or how to be a good friend. You have likely been told that you must be a friend to have a friend, but what does that mean? Did anyone hand you a book in middle school saying, "Here kid, this is what you need to know to be successful in relationships." No? Believe it or not, there *are* guidelines for how to have community in your life.

Proverbs 22:11 (ESV)
"He who loves purity of heart, and whose speech is gracious, will have the king as his friend."

4. Be a good friend in order to have a good friend.

Clearly, you must be a good friend to have a good friend. Everyone already knows that, right? However, it is important to understand that being a good friend does not guarantee you will have good friends. It only means you are choosing to control the part of the relationship that you have power over, yourself. People are attracted to people who make good friends. However, they may be attracted to you but that does not necessarily mean they will be a good friend.

What qualifies a good friend? How can you become a better friend? In high school I began picking up on cues pertaining to listening. Recognizing and appreciating the way certain people listened to me. I began to mimic what they did and since then I have consistently received compliments on being a good listener. Start with honing your listening skills to become a better friend. Be present when someone is speaking to you, do not interrupt. Respond well throughout the conversation with facial expressions and understanding nods. Learn what it takes to be a good listener and people will flock to you. Not all will be friends, but generally people will like you.

5. Friendship is give and take. It is not about wiping the slate clean but eliminating the slate completely.

We have some dear friends in our life that are incredibly generous with their time, resources, food, everything. They are constantly offering something to us, inviting us somewhere, or attempting to give us something. It is enjoyable to give and give and give not expecting anything in return. However, as soon as someone gives to me I feel indebted to them. As though I need to give back in such a way to even out the scoreboard. They invite us over for dinner, I set up a time to babysit for them. They help us move, I offer to bring a meal over. On and on the game goes. Turns out I have a receiving and scorekeeping problem. Good friends give *and* receive well. They do not keep score and attempt to even things out. They simply give and take continually to help and serve one another. They accept the gift graciously with a smile.

Ironically, in the midst of writing this chapter, these friends stepped up to the plate in a big way that challenged my slate breaking theory. Supposedly, moving is one of the top five most stressful things in life. Forget that. I can pack up our home in two days flat (granted there's only two of us and we have never lived in a home of more than 750 square feet). Home buying, on the other hand, is not for the faint of heart.

Marine Corps B.R.A.T.

It took us eight weeks from offer accepted to closing table on our first home. More alcohol was consumed and F-words said than any other season of my life. The closing date was moved seven times! Our mortgage broker was caught repeatedly lying and nearly blew the deal for us multiple times. Our current landlord was pleased that we kept him in the loop and had new tenants lined up for whenever we finally left. However, on a Friday he called to inform me that his realtor made a mistake, the new tenants were moving in on Monday. Three days later, *that* Monday. We had to be out. As I sat in the driveway after this news, crying under the stress, my girlfriend called to get the latest on the house-closing-saga. After a quick update it took only eight minutes for her husband to call me back and say, "Listen, I have a completely free day tomorrow so we are going to move all of your belongings into our garage and you guys will stay with us as long as you need to." Cue a fresh burst of tears. It took these friends just eight minutes to concoct and agree on this plan. No sleeping on it, pondering it, or mulling it over during dinner. We stayed at their place for two weeks, with every possession piled in their garage. *This* is friendship. *This* is community.

The first evening in their home, after showers, dinner and over a glass of whiskey I said, "We need to establish some ground rules because we want to chip in, not take advantage, and make sure we do not get in your way." Our friend held up his hand to stop me and said, "If this were your parents or a sibling would you have ever hesitated? Would you be saying this now? Would you feel bad or would this be expected because they are 'family'? *This* is what community is supposed to be. This is what we are called to do, how we are supposed to be to one another. To take care of each other. That is all we are doing here." He was absolutely right. Community is not only for Thanksgiving and Easter. They are supposed to be there to carry each other's burdens, to lend a helping hand, and to break the daggonne slate for good.

"You find out who your friends are
Somebody's gonna drop everything
Run out and crank up their car
Hit the gas get there fast
Never stop to think 'what's in it for me?' or 'it's way too far.'
They just show on up with their big old heart
You find out who you're friends are"
     - Find Out Who Your Friends Are by Tracy Lawrence

While this song has always been quality, it means exceedingly more when you find friends who genuinely "never stop to think 'what's in it for me' or 'it's way too far' but just show on up with their big old hearts".

Proverbs 17:17 (ESV)
"A friend loves at all times, and a brother is born for adversity."

6. Friendship takes root in similarities.

"Friendship ... is born at the moment when one man says to another "What! You too? I thought that no one but myself . . ." - C.S. Lewis

142

Marine Corps B.R.A.T.

My father-in-law was a professional at connecting with people. Upon introduction he would ask where you were from and manage to pull from his memory a story that occurred in that place. This usually left the person smiling or laughing. He connected. Find common ground with a stranger to make them feel more at ease and comfortable. That was his goal. When you know how to do this you never meet a stranger. People feel comfortable with you and will want to talk with you. Whether connecting for a brief moment to be a courteous host, or customer service representative or to find a lasting relationship, it is connections that draw people together.

Connections occur in a vast number of ways. Some connect by proximity (neighbors, co-workers), some because of similar interests (hobbies or career) and others due to beliefs, age, gender, kids, etc. One of my dearest friendships began only because we were the same age and newly married. Another friend I only see twice a year for business, however, we keep in touch from across the country mainly because of our beliefs and snarky sense of humor. As C.S. Lewis relates, friendship is based on a moment of connection with another person, a moment when you think "What?! You too??"

We may not all be like my father-in-law who sought connection with every person with whom he interacted. In fact, I most certainly was not like that until I realized I would be better at my job if I sharpened this skill. That is what it is, a craft or skill that can be learned. Some people are born with this innate skill and an overall love for people. Luckily, for the rest of us, it can be developed. After years, I now possess a mental quiver full of questions that help me connect with new people. Whether it is meeting people in my line of work, at church, an awkward social gathering or a party I did not particularly want to attend. Thanks to Dale Carnegie and training from Gary and Janet Googe (the sweetest southern couple who serve as another set of parents to us) I have learned that people simply want to be asked about themselves. People want to be heard. Allowing another person to talk causes them to feel cared about and that feeling activates connection.

On another note: for a few years I followed a well-known, respected female Christian author/speaker. Then she made a controversial statement that caused her books to be removed from shelves and had me questioning my following of her. I still enjoyed her snarky sense of humor, her "get to the heart of the matter" and "say it like it is" attitude. However, I struggled because of this single comment that reflected a core difference in our beliefs. After pondering this for a few weeks I finally asked my husband, "Can I still enjoy her and follow her but disagree with her on this item?" Yes! Yes, I can. In fact, I have found that I disagree with some of my dearest friends on some important issues, and it is okay. We can still be friends. They can still be our community. I can still love them, enjoy them, pour into them and allow them to do the same to/for me. Heck, I married a man that I disagree with daily and we are still making our relationship work. While friendships are formed and founded on similarities, they are built and maintained when two mature individuals can recognize differences and choose to press on.

7. Balance fun and intimacy.

Typically, men connect over activity and women over conversation. Women host home parties to chit chat and shop together while most men would rather be 20 yards from one another throwing a football without speaking a word. We connect differently. Within male/female differences there must be balance. We see this played out in marriage. A man may want to go for a bike ride, play a video game, go to a movie or mini-golfing while the woman simply wants a conversation. My husband wants to spend time with me even if that means not speaking. Watching his ass on a bicycle for a few miles is not helping me connect to him but it helps *him* connect to *me*. Returning home and discussing life, our dreams and the upcoming week over a glass of wine helps *me* connect with *him*. This balance in our relationship is important so that we both feel connected to one another and so we have activity *and* conversation. Too much of either hinders a deeper connection in the relationship. The same goes for friendships. Game nights are frequent in our current circle of friends. While I enjoy a game or two, I grow hungry for a meaningful conversation. Some of my fondest memories with friends have been when these two factors (activity and conversation) have been intertwined. When we are doing something we both enjoy (working out, shopping, taking a walk, etc.) while engaged in conversation. Every relationship needs this balance in order to connect on a deeper, emotional level.

8. Friendship is hard work, it is pursuing another human.

"You can't stay in your corner of the forest waiting for others to come to you. You have to go to them sometimes."
- Winnie the Pooh

During a season of moving and transition as a preteen, I was desperately trying to hang onto friendships I had left in Texas. Every Sunday (because this was back when weekend minutes were free for cell phones) I would call my three best friends to catch up. One weekend it occurred to me that I was always the one making these calls. I decided to not call and see what happened. Unfortunately, no one reached out. This little experiment went on a second weekend. Still no incoming calls. This is where I learned the difference between one-way and two-way friendships.

Friendship needs to be a two-way road, a space where two moving vehicles can come and go. A relationship should be give and take, both individuals caring for one another, asking questions, taking initiative, and pursuing the other. It is not easy. You must remember to be intentional. To gear up, put gas in the car, go out of your way, and sacrifice, to pursue another human. It takes effort. A one-way relationship, on the other hand, is one-sided. It is one person pursuing the other with no return effort. Often we do not realize we are in one of these relationships until we get frustrated with the person. Our expectations are not being met and we feel unloved and uncared for. All the miles are going onto our vehicle while the other is parked safely in the garage.

When you find a quality, two-way relationship, hang onto it! They are rare, and when someone cares for you the way you care for them, do not let go. Most one-way relationships need to be released. When you recognize that you are the only one pursuing, stop. When you have fewer or lower expectations on a person you will find more peace. Let that person go. It is okay. They are only frustrating you. Another consideration when presented with a one-way relationship is recognizing if there is a deeper, more important reason for your presence. When you discover your child is struggling and they are reluctant to confide in you, that is when you pursue the hardest. Even when you are not being pursued in return. Some people in our lives need us for a season. People who may not be capable of pursuing us in return but they need our help, wisdom, listening ear, etc. The best way to handle these relationships when you are presented with them is to identify them and set your expectations appropriately. When you expect a taker to ask about your life, day, dreams, or goals and they do not, you are the one left frustrated. Identify the truth of the relationship to appropriately set your expectations.

9. Boundaries = A circle of friends for seasons and reasons.

"Ever since the beginning to keep the world spinning
It takes all kinds of kinds, all kinds of kinds"
    - *All Kinds of Kinds* by Miranda Lambert

Have you ever experienced one person who calls you for everything? For every crisis you are on their speed dial, and it is exhausting? Every time you see their name you wonder what fire needs to be put out today? Eventually you no longer want to maintain this relationship. You pray for the day they make a new friend so that you do not have to serve as their all in all friendship.

During pre-marital counseling, we were told that we cannot and will not be able to be everything to each other. During dating and engagement phases it seems like you will be able to meet your spouse's every need. Impossible. Women need girlfriends to bond with differently than their husband. Men need time with the guys. We are wired differently and it is incredibly satisfying to connect with those that are like ourselves.

Two years into marriage, we began hosting and leading a home group through our church. We had about 12 people in their early 20's, most of whom were couples of all stages without children. That season was full of fun, 'doing life together' and impromptu hangouts. Eventually, I realized that while our peers were enjoyable, we did not have wisdom being spoken into us. I began feeling the need for a mentor, someone older than me that I could connect with and learn from. Community should be a collection, a variety of people in all stages of life, so you have multiple people to reach out to when life throws a curveball. A healthy circle of friends so that *you* are not the person draining the energy and life out of a single individual.

During sophomore year of high school, I invited two freshmen volleyball teammates to a few get-togethers. Expanding my circle of friends to have more than only my two closest friends. This did not bode well for me. Those original two became very bitter towards this choice, and those friendships ended. To this day, (maybe because of that experience, maybe not) it still bothers me when girls refer to someone as their "best friend." It rubs me the wrong way. Why do we put this title on someone? That is so much pressure for a single individual to live up to! The title implies that this is your person, your go to, your non replaceable, and worst of all, that there is only one. When I hear it there is a pang of jealousy mixed with sadness. Jealousy, often because I feel close enough to be given that title, but they spoke it in front of me in reference to someone else. Sadness for the person speaking because they do not have a circle. They do not have a posse. They have '_A_ best friend.'

Personally, I am continually cultivating an ensemble of "best friends." However, I cannot count on a single one of them for _everything_. The advantage of multiple close friendships is that they are _drastically_ easier to maintain. When there is a collection of people it is not assumed that you will be someone else's all in all. When there is a team of people around you there is variety, wisdom, perspective, and entertainment. Currently, my circle consists of about 12 women ranging from ages 23 to 67 in about eight different states. We certainly cannot "do life together" because of the physical distance. However, distance does not lessen the bond. Distance does not prevent these women to be available for me through thick and thin. However, they are not all available at once. And that is okay, even healthy.

The best way to convey this principle is to read the book *Boundaries,* by Dr. Henry Cloud. It is said that a few close friends should be preferred to a mass of acquaintances. Yes, you do not and should not bare your heart and soul to a mass of people. However, be a friend collector. When you find a good one, keep them! You do not have to get rid of one because you have added another. Be a friend to them so they want to keep you as well. Build a circle of confidants around you and be the friend you want to procure. You will be amazed at what your circle will begin to look like and the support with which you will have surrounded yourself.

"Make new friends,
But keep the old.
One is silver,
The other is gold."
- Unknown

10. Average of Five.

"You are the average of the five people you spend the most time with." - Jim Rohn

"Friends should cause you to grow, sometimes that means moving on." - Unknown

Writing this chapter I found an article that expressed why "the average of five" concept is incorrect. The article conveyed how the statement is not accurate and a number of reasons as to why. Whether the nitty gritty of the quote is true or not, the overall message is to put things into perspective. How are you selecting those you spend time with? Who is being given permission to have influence over your life? Are you allowing someone to stay in a position of influence or are they residing there by default? Default relationships mean your life is coasting. You are riding the waves of what comes at you without input. You are playing the role of a victim. More than likely you cannot trade in all of your co-workers that you are around daily. Instead, how can you be the influencer in that setting rather than the influenced?

A teenager with incredibly strong opinions and a deep, con-victing, moral compass was once asked, "But what about peer pressure?" The young man confidently replied, "Sir, I am the peer pressure." Are you that confident and sure of yourself? Wherever you stand on "being" the peer pressure, the influencer, the people around you *will* have an impact on who you are.

Recently, I became fast friends with a new peer from church. Six months later she decided to move to Boston for a change of atmosphere. After many of the arrangements had been made, at the last minute she changed her mind and backed out. Sharing the glad news with me she gave her reason for the sudden change of heart. She said, "I asked myself, will this move, this change, help me become the person I want to be, or will staying here around these new friends do that?" She decided to stay. To be honest, it absolutely felt like a little gold star on my imaginary sash. More importantly though, this indicates that we have surrounded ourselves with quali-ty people, and that others see it and want to be a part.

Who are your five people?

Besides my husband, often, my five people are not local. They are friends that I spend copious amounts of time with on the phone. Your five people do not have to be nose to nose with you to count.

Life changes every six months. Something drastic could happen, a new habit may develop, you might become a completely different person. Whatever it is, your life is likely going to change in some way every six months. Take stock of your five people about that frequently. Are they the same? Do you enjoy them? Do they challenge you? Are the relationships edifying? Do you want to grow in the same direction that they are growing? If not, change them. You can do that. Do not passively watch your life drift by. Choose the people you want in your circle.

John 15:13 (ESV)
"Greater love has no one than this, that someone lay down his life for his friends."

Finally, choose to focus on serving and caring about others. However simple, those skills are the foundation of any good relationship. To surround ourselves with great people we have to be aware of who we are around, who we spend time with, how we are coming across to others, and how we can serve them well. I highly recommend reading Dale Carnegie's book *How to Win Friends and Influence People*. Recently, my husband gave me the sweetest compliment during a group discussion. As two others expressed their difficulty with relationships due to being wired as task-focused individuals, my husband shared how I balance this. He said I am the most task-focused person he has ever met, and yet, when put in a given situation I manage to balance the task at hand *while* caring for people. By intentionally asking questions and getting to know people, while still getting the job done. While this was of the highest of compliments, I share it so you understand that you do not have to be the "people-est" of people persons to build quality relationships. You can be naturally task-focused and still learn to care for and serve others well. Everything in this chapter can be learned. Nothing in this book is something you or I were born with and those that were not are screwed. It can all be learned and applied. If you do not currently have quality people around you, I understand. However, know that it is only a season (or it can be). You can apply these principles, learn to be a better friend yourself, and seek out quality people to "do life with" right now. You can choose to build your own community.

How to Win Friends and Influence People
Principles:

- Don't criticize, condemn or complain
- Give honest and sincere appreciation
- Arouse in the other person an eager want
- Become genuinely interested in other people
- Smile
- Remember that a person's name is to that person the sweetest and most important sound in any language
- Be a good listener. Encourage others to talk about themselves
- Talk in terms of the other person's interests
- Make the other person feel important – and do it sincerely
- Win people to your way of thinking
- The only way to get the best of an argument is to avoid it
- Show respect for the other person's opinions. Never say, "You're wrong"
- If you are wrong, admit it quickly and emphatically
- Begin in a friendly way
- Get the other person saying "yes, yes" immediately
- Let the other person do a great deal of the talking

- Let the other person feel that the idea is his or hers
- Try honestly to see things from the other person's point of view
- Be sympathetic with the other person's ideas and desires
- Appeal to the nobler motives
- Dramatize your ideas
- Throw down a challenge
- Be a Leader: How to Change People Without Giving Offense or Arousing Resentment
- Begin with praise and honest appreciation
- Call attention to people's mistakes indirectly
- Talk about your own mistakes before criticizing the other person
- Ask questions instead of giving direct orders
- Let the other person save face
- Praise the slightest improvement and praise every improvement. Be "hearty in your approbation and lavish in your praise"
- Give the other person a fine reputation to live up to
- Use encouragement. Make the fault seem easy to correct
- Make the other person happy about doing the thing you suggest

Marine Corps B.R.A.T.

Keep Growing:
How to Win Friends and Influence People
by Dale Carnegie
Boundaries by Dr. Henry Cloud
Personality Plus by Florence Littauer

9. Faith

"'According to your faith be it unto you.' - Matthew 9:29 The requirement is faith, and directly in proportion to the faith that you have and use will you get results."
   - *The Power of Positive Thinking*
   by Norman Vincent Peale

"When we are once again convinced of the importance of God's help in our activities, then true progress will have been accomplished."
   - *The Power of Positive Thinking*
   by Norman Vincent Peale

My mom would not allow us to own Disney's interpretation of the movie *Hercules*...We were allowed to watch it but not own it. *Confused shrug* We will never understand all our parent's rules. *Hercules* may have been my earliest exposure to Greek mythology, although my fascination with it began with my first reading of *The Odyssey* and *The Iliad* in middle school. Whenever it was offered on a reading list for an assignment I would choose *The Odyssey* yet again. By the end of high school I had read it three times. One of my English courses was completely on Greek mythology. I love these myths.

Greek/Roman mythology is unique compared to other ancient mythologies. Before my husband and I took a celebratory trip to Ireland I attempted to read book on Irish mythology and wound up abandoning it. The stories lacked a certain luster and there were too many Gaelic names I could not pronounce. It did not have the same draw as my beloved Greek characters do. When the first Percy Jackson movie was released my friend suggested I read the books. Initially, I was under the impression they were for children and would be corny for me to read as an adult. I was wrong. The next time my friend came over he brought the entire series and I was finished in less than three months, making me very popular with my 10 year old nephew.

While Greek mythology is captivating from a story standpoint, what jumps out to me on a deeper level are the blatant character flaws. Epic stories of heroes who save the day and yet inevitably make one wrong move, one poor choice that ends in their demise. Usually it is a long, drawn out story of inconceivable challenges leading to incredible victory and before you know it, the hero has made one reckless choice ending their life and the story.

We expect this of humans. Even revered heroes of today, people of incredible talent, grit, leadership, fame, fortune, etc. We all know that they are human and likely going to let us down. Disappointing, but expected. What stands out in these stories are the imperfections and flaws of the gods and goddesses.

Marine Corps B.R.A.T.

We were raised in a non-denominational church (oxymoron I know). I rededicated my life to Christ 37 times by the age of nine. Baptized at age 11, I won seventh place in a scripture memorization contest, and was on the worship team through sixth grade. Church was a second home for most of my childhood, and it was great! We were taught to believe in the one true God, His son Jesus Christ, and the Holy Spirit that fills us today, forming the Holy Trinity.

My parents encouraged us to wrestle with these truths, to make our belief in Christianity our own and I did a lot of questioning as a preteen. Never with much doubt of the truth of it all, simply seeking more understanding. In high school and college I took World Religions classes. My parents never hid other religions or beliefs from me. They were spoken of openly in our home and our questions were always answered candidly. These religion classes gave me an in-depth look at what other people believed and why. It was also interesting to get an outsider's take on my own belief system.

For those who have not taken a class on World Religions, here is your extremely brief rundown:
There are 5 major, dominating religions in the world today:
1. Christianity
2. Judaism
3. Islam
4. Buddhism
5. Hinduism

Christianity: Founded on the primary belief that God sent his only Son, Jesus Christ, to die a horrendous death on the cross and then rise from the dead in order to pay for the sins of humans that they may have the choice to spend eternity in Heaven. God, Jesus, and the Holy Spirit make up the Holy Trinity, God, three-in-one.

Judaism: Christianity and Islam both stem from the same history as Judaism. Christianity broke away from Judaism when they believed that Jesus Christ was the long awaited Messiah. Jews believed Jesus was not the Son of God. They believe in the one God of their ancestors but are still waiting for the coming Messiah promised to them in scriptures.

Islam: Based on the teachings of the prophet Muhammad. Muslims believe in one god called Allah and that their acts (good or bad) on earth will determine what kind of reward they will receive in the afterlife (if any).

Buddhism: Based on the teachings of Gautama, the Buddha. Primary focus and beliefs of loving without conditions, compassion for others, sympathetic joy, impartiality, and reincarnation based on each life's actions or good deeds to-wards others.

Hinduism: Believes in thousands of gods with one supreme being, Brahman. The goal is to one day reach a level of "goodness" to be worthy of being united with Brahman, un-til then, to be reincarnated repeatedly.

This is clearly the simplest, most generalized run-down of the beliefs of each of these five major religions. After this extremely simplified cliff notes of religion we can see three unique factors that set Christianity apart from the others. While the other four religions focus heavily on what each individual must *do* to reach "success," Christianity negates that. Christianity focuses on what God did *for* us. In addition, Christianity provides a God who sacrificed *for* us rather than our sacrificing for Him. No other religion replicates this or has a founder who rose from the dead. Finally, the third major difference is that, within Christianity, we are given a choice. Our "success" is not dependent on our actions, or on a wishful whim that we have done enough good to outweigh our bad deeds. Instead, if we simply believe in who Jesus was and what He did for us we will experience "success" in our "religion." That success being the opportunity to spend eternity in Heaven with God. The other religions rely on ourselves, our good deeds, and a hopeful wish that we will have made the cut when this life ends.

Christianity offers a God, a Savior who took the form of a human in order to die to cover all our sins so that we might have the option to spend eternity in Heaven. No other religion has a god that sacrifices himself for the good of his creation. No other religion has a god that loves enough to do such a thing. And no other religion requires so little of you than Christianity. Instead of my fate, the determination of where I spend eternity relying on me and my actions, it all relies on Christ and what He already did for me. All I have to do, is believe in that truth. Seems *too* easy, right?

Growing up believing in one, perfect, loving, sacrificial God is comforting, to say the least. There is peace in confidently knowing that my mistakes, my poor choices, not a single act I commit can mess with His plan. Believing that He has it all worked out, that He has the very best plan for me, that everything He does is in my very best interest. This divine perfection and power over everything provides one with incredible peace. The relationship of God with us is often compared to that of a father and children. While we do not always understand why Mom will let us watch *Hercules* but not own it, if we take a moment to think, we know she has our very best interest at heart. Her sole purpose for any rules is to protect and provide us with a life of love and fulfillment. The same is true with our Heavenly Father.

Returning to the Greek myths may seem silly to you, but stick with me. While you may know someone who believes in Buddhism, Hinduism, or Islam, likely you do not know anyone who prays to Zeus about the weather or Demeter concerning infertility. Yet, for thousands of years people believed in these gods and goddesses. They believed that they not only controlled or affected, but also meddled in their day to day lives.

Just for fun, in case you are not familiar with the main Greek gods and goddesses, here is a brief review:

- Zeus: King of the gods, god of weather, law and fate
- Hera: Queen of the gods, goddess of women, marriage and childbirth
- Aphrodite: goddess of beauty and love

- Apollo: god of the sun, truth, prophesy, knowledge, music, poetry, dance and healing
- Ares: god of war
- Artemis: goddess of the moon, hunting, animals and childbirth
- Athena: goddess of wisdom, art, war and defense
- Demeter: goddess of agriculture, grain and fertility
- Hephaestus: god of fire, volcanoes, blacksmiths, metalworking, craft-workers and sculpture
- Hermes: god of travel, hospitality, business, weights and measures and sport
- Poseidon: god of the sea, earthquakes and horses
- Hestia: goddess of home, hearth and family
- Hades: god of the underworld

With 12 gods on Mount Olympus running the world, you would think they would have the earth under some sort of control. I mean, there are 12 of them! You would assume they cared about what is going on in their realm and these humans they created. Instead, they are constantly causing trouble amongst themselves and with the people of earth. Pitting humans against one another, falling in love with humans resulting in offspring called demigods and getting involved with human conflict in an effort to avenge some wrong committed against them. Like a pack of 12 siblings playing a game with no consequences except that their toys are living beings. There is humor and tragedy in these stories but the underlying theme I cannot escape when I read them is that people believed it. People would pray to certain gods or goddesses for guidance or assistance. They believed that gods could be pitted against them. How stressful!! To never know when something you might have done could anger or irritate a powerful being. To be unsure who is on your side or what god might be tampering with your life circumstances. Can you fathom living this way? I imagine it would cause you to live a cautious, not to mention, superstitious life. Always in uncertainty and a little bit of turmoil.

While these tales are only stories from long ago, there are religions still practiced today that can be very similar to these myths. These religions or beliefs may not have a long list of gods to pray to or be wary of, but they may believe in an all powerful god who is out to get them. While many people are raised to believe in a certain religion, ultimately it is each individual's choice to decide what they believe. There may be people out there choosing to pray to Zeus, I don't know. Certainly, we have all met someone choosing to believe there is no supreme being or higher power at all. However, some choose to believe in religions that represent a god that is not on their side. A god that is waiting for them to mess up, to punish them, waiting to say, "I told you so." Standing by to sentence them to damnation, and therefore, causing these believers to live lives in uncertainty and a constant state of inner turmoil.

"Human history is the long terrible story of man trying to find something other than God which will make him happy." - C.S. Lewis

Thankfully, in this life, we have choices. While my parents raised us to believe a certain way they never pushed, shoved, or demanded belief from us. The choice was always ours. They encouraged us to seek and find truth for ourselves. Some families are not so encouraging or forgiving. It can be hard to offer that freedom to someone you love when they choose a direction that is different from yours. However, offering freedom demands a level of faith and trust that I believe only God can provide.

You have a choice. Whatever your family situation, how you were raised, or what you think you believe right now, you still have a choice. You can choose to continue believing as you do, continue to be indifferent about how you believe, or choose to challenge your beliefs and seek more knowledge. Living in America, we have freedom, without condemnation (for the time being anyhow…) to study all religions, to learn everything about them and select which one to live our life by. Your beliefs are between you and God. I have no intention of spending this chapter persuading you to believe a certain way. However, because this is *my* book we are going to review more about Jesus through the lens of ancient Greek mythology.

If you have ever studied earth origin stories, myths, or religions you know that people, will believe almost anything. Greek mythology certainly does not contain the craziest stories that humans have put their faith and trust in. While these gods and goddesses are horribly flawed and imperfect (much like ourselves as humans) there are a few more characteristics that cause me to be even more grateful for *my* God.

1. They are not all-knowing

My God, part of the Holy Trinity, the Father of Jesus Christ, who died on the cross for my sins, He does not sleep. He is always awake, always part of what is going on in every crevice of the earth. He is in your life and mine across the world at the same time. He sees everything, has a hand on everything and a plan for everything. Nothing can be hidden from Him, no secrets or shame. However, the gods of Mount Olympus hide things from each other! They can be tricked by mortal humans, and they can keep secrets from one another. They do not always know where their husband is. They require sleep. They can be tricked and lied to. They are not all seeing, all knowing beings. They are limited much like we are. *My* God does not have limitations. He is on call for any one of His creations and no thought or action can be hidden from Him. When we make mistakes it is usually difficult to admit. However, when someone clearly saw the mistake occur it is easier to discuss our actions and move forward. It is a blessing to know that the Lord of all creation knows my heart, my every thought, and action. Before I share it with Him, He has seen it, He is aware, and He has already forgiven me.

2. They can experience fear

Kronos, the Titan who fathered Zeus, was fearful that one of his children would dethrone him. Therefore, he ate his newborn children in an effort to prevent this. Later, Zeus experienced this same fear and swallowed one of his wives to prevent one of her children from dethroning him. This is outrageous, kind of silly, and obviously unrealistic (but they are myths so they can do what they want). However, it shows at the very beginning of these stories, from the patriarch of the gods of Olympus, fear was present. It seems that when you are not an all knowing, all powerful, never sleeping being you are doomed to a level of uncertainty and therefore, fear.

While *my* God experiences many emotions: sadness, joy, anger, and certainly jealousy, fear is never present. Fear is mentioned in the Bible 365 times. Not to document the Lord's fear, rather commanding us to "fear not."
As a child, when there is a monster under the bed or in the closet and your dad appears, he removes your fear. You trust him when he says there is no monster and no reason to fear. You believe that he is telling the truth and that he is "all knowing" about monsters. You are confident that if you call, he is going to answer and he will interrupt his sleep to comfort you. That is how the Heavenly Father functions as well. Whatever the fear or uncertainty is, we can call on Him *anytime* and He is there. He is ready to be Dad and still all fears.

3. Choice of belief

In most creation stories or myths, we find people blindly putting faith in whatever they were taught to believe. Surely, someone questioned these beliefs but we have no record of that. Likely, displaying unbelief in a small, tightly knit community of believers long ago would get you into trouble.

Today, we have an abundance of options, and in America we are free to select from those options. We can worship openly without being ridiculed, study without hindrance and question without being shamed (for the most part). However with choice comes freedom for which we are responsible. It is our responsibility to choose something to believe. Personally, I believe agnostics are lazy. To be an agnostic means you do not care enough to invest time or effort into understanding what is out there and what you believe. It is a state of indifference. The counter argument may be that an agnostic simply cannot be confident of a deity, a specific higher power, and therefore, view their agnostic stance as acknowledging their lack of knowledge: there is something out there but I am unsure of what it is. If this is you, I encourage you to do some research, ponder your options, understand what you believe and want to bet your eternity on. Whatever you do, choose *something*. When you believe that there is life after death that lasts for eternity (which is a really, really long time), you better believe you will do your due diligence in figuring out what that looks like.[17]

"A young man who wishes to remain a sound atheist [*insert: agnostic*] cannot be too careful of his reading." - C.S. Lewis

"Christianity, if false, is of no importance, and if true, of infinite importance. The only thing it cannot be is moderately important." - C.S. Lewis

---

[17] https://relevantmagazine.com/culture/film/how-lee-strobel-tried-to-disprove-god-and-failed/

4. Faithful

Faithfulness is: loyal, constant, dedicated, and steadfast.

- Mother Earth and Sky produced 12 children called the Titans. Mother Earth informed her child, Kronos, that his son would dethrone him. What she did not tell him was that his wife would trick him causing this downfall. Mother Earth was not faithful to her child in this matter. Rhea, Kronos' wife, was not faithful in telling him the truth in an effort to prevent him from eating one of her children.
- In one example of Zeus and Hera's rocky relationship: Zeus had other wives and Hera was jealous whenever he was away from her. Once, he fell in love with a human named Io and had to turn her into a cow in an effort to hide her from Hera's wrath.
- Zeus' first wife, Metis, he swallowed to prevent her from having a son that would dethrone him.
- There were five ages of humans created. In the beginning, Zeus alone created these humans. The first, the Golden Age, died off. The second, the Silver Age, Zeus merely grew tired of and destroyed them. The third, the Bronze Age, contained warriors who fought and killed each other. The fourth, the Heroic Age is when Zeus finally acquired some help from Prometheus, Athena, and Mother Earth. As you can see, he made these creations and cared nothing for them. When he grew weary of them, he destroyed them without remorse, love, or concern. How would you

like to live knowing the king of the gods could simply grow weary of your race and wipe you out completely?[18]

Thankfully, *my* God is ever faithful. We find story after story in the Bible of Israelites (God's "chosen" people) disobeying His commands, slandering Him and blatantly acting against His wishes. They are repeatedly unfaithful to Him. However, again and again, He welcomes them back into His good graces. He forgives them and reassures them that He is their God, He is ever faithful, and He will never forsake them. There are consequences for every action and choices, but never could the Israelites do so much wrong that the Lord forsook them completely. Just as a loving father could never completely forsake His child, the God of all creation is ever faithful to us.

5. Perfection

The Greek gods and goddesses were imperfect. They fought with each other, meddled in humanity and constantly sought to satisfy their own desires. Thank God *my* God loves

---

[18] *Disclaimer: Yes, God did cause a flood during the time of Noah (about 2500 B.C.) wiping out all but eight people. At face value this may appear similar to Zeus' action. With minimal study we find the only statement about Zeus' reasoning was having "grown weary" of the people. He got bored. The God of Noah had warned His people about sinning against His commands over and over again. He created humans with a purpose, not only for His own entertainment. They were given specific guidelines on how to conduct themselves. Simply put, there were consequences for their actions, their disobedience against the God that created them and that is what caused God to flood the earth.

us more than that. He loves us more than His own desires. He certainly did not *want* to send His only Son to die on a cross and surely it wrecked Him when His Son cried out to Him, feeling utterly forsaken by Him. However, He endured that painful experience because it meant that you and I can live with Him for eternity in Heaven. In addition to eternal bliss, because of His sacrifice, you and I get to experience a personal relationship with the Creator of the universe while living life on earth.

Life on earth is one matter, but eternity is a really long time. What are you going to put *your* trust in?

If being a large family of homeschooled kids and moving across the country every few years did not label our family "weird," we threw in Christianity as icing on the cake. While some southern homeschooled kids were not permitted to explore mythology or origin stories other than what the Bible contained, our parents shared openly with us and allowed us to question everything. Ironically, studying Greek mythology only drew me to a deeper and more committed relationship with my Lord.

There are books filled with more on this information and containing every viewpoint you can imagine, I have only scratched the surface. However, as you read this chapter, what did it spark inside of you? Did you learn something new about faith, religion or Greek mythology? Are you freaked out by my fascination with Greek mythology or my Christian upbringing? I encourage you to keep going, do not stop here. If this chapter stirred you then please dig in a little more. Research, explore your faith. Why do you believe what you believe? What does it all mean for you?

"If I find in myself a desire which no experience in this world can satisfy, the most probable explanation is that I was made for another world." - C.S. Lewis

Keep Growing:
The Case for Christ by Lee Strobel
Know Why You Believe by Paul E. Little
Living Religions by Mary Pat Fisher
Ancient Greece Gods and Goddesses by John Malam
God Space by Doug Pollock
The Ragamuffin Gospel by Brennan Manning

10. Service & Sacrifice

"Your true character is most accurately measured by how you treat those who can do nothing for you."
- Mother Teresa

"It's not about how much you do, but how much love you put into what you do that counts." - Mother Teresa

"Life's most persistent and urgent question is, 'What are you doing for others?'" - Martin Luther King Jr.

For her 50th birthday my mom requested the whole family spend a weekend volunteering at a YoungLife camp. She was so excited to share a serving opportunity with her family. This is the kind of stuff my mom lives for. Unfortunately, she had a bratty 19 year old child who sucked the joy out of it for her. *This* is what you want to do for your birthday?! For your 50th?! You want us to balance trays of food, fill glasses, and clean up nasty, half eaten plates for three days? Ew! Gross! Regrettably, I cannot say I walked away from that experience with a new perspective on serving others. Or even a decent attitude towards it. Instead, I left that camp irritated over the whole situation. It took a lot of years for me to begin grasping the importance of service in my life.

Marine Corps B.R.A.T.

It is embarrassing to admit that, as old as I was, my attitude towards serving others was so lousy. Even more shaming is the stink I made of the family outing that my mom was so excited about for her birthday. Kids are awful. Maybe right now you feel the way I did about serving. You think "Ew, gross." What is the point? Shouldn't people help themselves? If my attitude had not changed towards serving I would not be writing this. Certainly, I am not living the most sacrificial of lives and not to imply a self righteous better than you air. Rather, I have been where you are and luckily, I have learned a little since then. That is what writing and/or teaching is, being one tiny step ahead, or knowing 10% more than the audience. Here I am, I do not have anything mastered but this is what I have to offer, and I hope it helps you.

Maybe you are frustrated with the idea of sacrificing yourself for someone else. Perhaps you have an underlying, moral compass in you that pressures you to live more sacrificially. Why can people not all simply help themselves? Why should I clean up someone's yard when it appears they could afford a landscaper? Why would I serve food at a camp when it seems they could manage waitstaff? Why should I stop my life to assist someone on the side of the road? Their problem is not my problem. Right?

However, *that* is the problem, we do not get it! We may never fully understand. Serving is a strange concept. When we choose to serve, it can make us feel really good about ourselves. When we are forced to serve, we may harbor feelings of resentment towards the experience. And when we try to serve for the sheer sake of serving, we may experience guilt for feeling good about ourselves when the goal was to do something for someone else. Serving and sacrificing is peculiar and mysterious.

In an episode of the TV show *Friends,* sweet, sacrificial Phoebe attempts to do something kind for another being that brings her absolutely no joy or good feelings. To prove her point that goodness can be done for the sheer sake of goodness, she finally allows a bee to sting her. After a triumphant sting she discovers the bee will likely now die because of that sting. Even when we try to serve for that sake of serving, it seems we cannot. Are we really serving someone else or is it always self serving to serve others?

The cycle of serving may not make sense, but we can be confident that serving and sacrificing for others is *good*. It is good for whoever you are serving and it is good for your own heart and soul. Whether or not you believe in the Bible, most religions support this theory. We ought to love and serve others sacrificially. Likely, you can think of a time when you did something good for someone else and it felt good for you both. Maybe it was not that one time your mom dragged you up a mountain for a weekend to serve food to campers. Rather, it may have been when you gave someone your spot in line, turned in a lost wallet, or let someone in on the highway. You have likely served somebody in your lifetime and experienced gratification afterwards.

Serving should not have to be confusing, frustrating or obligating. It certainly *can* be those things but it does not *have* to be. What it does have to be is intentional…for most of us. There are personalities that have a giving feature wired into them. For the rest of us we must understand *why* serving is worth the effort and learn how to be intentional to incorporate it into our lives. Similar to reading, if all you have ever read is fiction or you struggle with reading altogether, why would you be intentional about incorporating more of it into your life? You would need to understand how reading would positively impact you in order to make a change to do it more. The same goes for serving.

What is the purpose of serving and / or sacrificing?

Serve: *to act as a servant*
Sacrifice: *to surrender or give up, or permit injury or disadvantage to, for the sake of something else.* (dictionary.com)

Why act as a servant? The Bible frequently directs us to serve others (Biblical directions are always meant for the betterment of our lives). However, to provide the simplest possible answer: because it feels good for you and helps others.

Serving is a gift of action. It is giving to someone else while at the same time sacrifice is removing something from you. Sacrifice is to give up one thing for that of another. Today I gave up some sleep to get up at 5:30 and spend time writing before my dog decided it is playtime. Some days I give up extra writing time for more sleep. Sacrifice can go either way. We can sacrifice something good for something not so good or something mediocre for something so much better. In fact, most of us tend to sacrifice the *best* for *good* or even just *OK* and coast through our lives rather than sacrificing *fine* for the *best*.

When my parents informed us that we would be moving to a summer camp for homeless and inner-city kids to run the place year round I had a meltdown. My younger siblings were stoked (and to be honest, they are all much better people than I am). My 12 year old self was terrified that my desires were going to be neglected and these "other people's" needs put before my own. My parents were not asking me, they were telling me that I was about to begin living a more sacrificial life and I was not about it. Distinctly, I remember this meltdown and a specific conversation with my mom. Surely, she sat there wondering where she had gone wrong with me. Sorry Mom. Despite *my* feelings, frustrations and concerns, we moved. Apparently preteens do not get much input about when and where the family moves. The camp sessions were never my favorite. It was a struggle for me to connect with the kids in attendance. However, I did my part helping and serving behind the scenes in administrative roles (those were the roles I got to be *in charge* of something and being in charge has always been my *forte*). Did I come away with a heart of service? Nope. We moved from that camp and I thought "This is freedom from that burden for my family." Did I sacrifice during that season? Yes. Was I happy about it? No. Would I have changed it in the moment? Absolutely. Would I change it now? Probably not.

That property and experience were priceless. My siblings and I had a ball there. However, it was a lot of work and stress on everyone and none of us would be who we are today without that experience. Heck, when my husband and I purchased our first home, built in 1870, it was *way* less scary after having lived in a 120 year old farmhouse on that camp that was practically falling down. My 1870 home is like a treasure compared to that "experienced" building.

This was sacrificial living. Like it or not, we did it. We all sacrificed and learned, via on the job training, how to live a lifestyle of service. Most people do not get this kind of up-bringing or experience. It is extremely outlandish. However, I know folks whose kids have hearts of gold and are constantly fundraising to help others in need. That was not me as a kid and maybe that is something we grow out of. Maybe, because we do not have responsibilities as children, we have more bandwidth to focus on others. Perhaps we get scarred by adulthood or politics and wonder why everyone cannot fend for themselves or why the government is not picking up the slack. However, the fact is, it is not up to the government, churches, or the non-profits. It is up to us. When the government tosses a handout to someone in need does the individual sincerely value it? Possibly. Yet, when you or I consciously sacrifice something in our own lives, our money or our time, how much more does that speak to someone in need? How much more appreciative are they that you would choose to do this for them? You have the power to make a positive, impactful difference in the life of someone else…that is *why* serving and sacrificing is important.

It is important to realize that *you* are not supposed to serve and sacrifice for *everyone*. There are some personalities (ahem…my mom) who want to do this. They want to help everyone they possibly can. While that may seem noble and good, it is actually exhausting and unrealistic. You must ask yourself, who matters to you? Not in a way that disregards everyone else, but consider a category of people. What group, or type of people make your heart ache? Whom do you want to see a change in their situation the most?

Were you ever asked what makes you angry or what makes you cry? Maybe it was specific to my upbringing, but I was asked these questions a lot in and around high school. "Finding your passion" is something much of my generation is hung up on. Passions change, just pick something and move forward. I digress…what makes you angry? What makes you cry?

Since a very young age it has upset me that there are children in the world who are not given the opportunity to simply be children. My parents always told us "Be a kid for as long as you can." This did not mean to live at home forever and never get real jobs or grow up. Their point was, do not rush into things. Enjoy this short season of your life, you will get to be a grown-up forever. I took that kind of stuff to heart. When I realized there were kids who have to work to contribute to their family's basic needs and do not get three meals a day or get to play or read etc. that bothers me. It is not fair that even struggling Americans have so much more than those in other parts of the world. As a teenager, I never understood when the opportunity came up to "sponsor-a-child" in a third-world country why all the adults were not sponsoring three or four. I thought, "Can you really not manage to give those kids $100 a month rather than just $30 for only one?" Thus, a passion for international adoption was borne inside of me and has brewed for years.

What is it for you? What is it in the world that makes you righteously angry or makes you want to cry? How can you serve those people? Or what experience have you been through that you understand in a way that most people do not? My mom dealt with infertility almost immediately after my parents got married. As a result of this struggle she can be an understanding ear and offer sound advice to those in the same boat. What part of your story can you use to serve others?

What skill do you have? My dad does not *enjoy* working on broken down vehicles, but he certainly knows his way around them. If someone is on the side of the road needing gas, a jump, or a tire change he is right there to assist them. When someone needs help budgeting or making a healthy meal plan my husband and I offer our assistance.

Recently a group from our church was challenged to serve someone in our community. To be honest, I was not thrilled about it. First, taking time out of my schedule in the busiest month of my year was stressful. Second, someone was supposed to assist us in finding this "serving opportunity" but they did not and finding the opportunity fell to my shoulders (taking *more* of my time). Third, the best I could find in the given timeframe and lack of resources was cleaning an elderly gentleman's yard. I am fully capable of raking and bagging leaves. Is this my passion, does my heart ache for

this man's leafy autumn yard? Not at all. Have I been
through this tough experience of a messy yard that better
equips me to help this man? I mean…I guess? Or is cleaning
up yards in my special skills set? I am capable…do I love it?
No. Sometimes that is what serving is. It is simply helping
someone because you are capable when they are not. This 90
year old man thanked us profusely for our time, but also for
our able bodies. It is thought provoking to be thanked for
your sheer ability to stand in a yard and rake leaves. It
makes you a little more grateful for your health and
strength.

When it comes to who you should serve, look around you.
You might find you can use your skills, experiences, or passions, or you might just find somebody that could use a
hand that you have to offer.

During our discussion about this serving project our church
group did, someone made a comment that irked me. She
stated that we would not find a family "in-need" this holi-
day season within our given town. That, in order to serve or
bless a family "in-need" we would have to look outside of
our town. Are you kidding me?! You truly believe there is
not a single family in our town that we could serve or bless?
I just called four different non-profit organizations *within* our
town, two of which were soup kitchens. Okay, so we do not
live in a poor area or downtown anything, but there are
homeless and struggling people everywhere. You just have
to look for them!

If you think there is no one to serve in your area, you have your eyes closed. Yes, I had to make four calls to find that single serving opportunity, but I was on a time crunch. What non-profits are in your community? A quick google search will give you a list. Who are your neighbors? Do you know them and what their lives are about? Maybe the person next door needs what you have to offer. Do not be fooled by thinking that someday in the future you will have more time to devote to serving others. You never will, that is a myth. Recently I read a meme that said, "Adulthood is just saying 'but after this week things will slow down' until you die." Do not be fooled that you will one day have "more time." Open your eyes and look around you for where you can serve and help people now.

My parents have always lived a life of service, putting other's needs above their own. They are constantly helping others. They do not even have to seek it out, other people's needs somehow find them. My dad does not even consider whether or not to stop and help someone on the side of the road, he just does it. My mom will sacrifice sleeping, eating, mental and physical health, whatever it takes to ensure people are taken care of. Throughout my life at home (and since then) we had many people live with our family when they were struggling. In fact, my husband's family lived with ours briefly when we were children and they suddenly became homeless. My mom said to me, "We could have been in their shoes a month ago and would have wanted someone to do the same for us." The seven of us kids had a ball! Navigating cooking, cleaning, and clashing personalities for the adults was a different story, but the offspring were blissfully oblivious.

Another way my parents served was to their country through the Marine Corps. Serving as a Marine for 11 years, my dad grasped service and sacrifice from a military stance. Even though the time of his service was mostly during times of peace for the United States, he still sacrificed. My mom still sacrificed. We, as a family, sacrificed. My dad's position required that he be gone for six months at a time. This made for awkward reunions and getting reacquainted each return. Prior to smart phones and the internet so when he missed a childhood milestone, he really missed it. It was not that he "missed it" by being absent and experiencing it on a screen. It was a moment gone forever. Before GPS, my mom had to plant the family in a new location, load us into the car and drive around the area, getting very lost in order to learn her new surroundings. My parents sacrificed for the freedom of our country. While it was hard, neither of them would go back and change it. This was service to a country. That is a little hard to grasp, it is not just a flag or a pledge, it is to an entire people that live there. That live *here*. My parents served for every single resident of the United States of America. They sacrificed precious family moments for the betterment, and safety of a people. That is a lot of sacrifice. That is why we recognize our military (and their families) for their efforts. They are putting aside their own desires for the good of others. Now that is noble.

A final note on serving: while serving and sacrificing for others can seem warm, fuzzy, and kind of squishy, there is also some serious pay-off. Andy Horner (co-founder of Premier Designs Inc.) repeatedly said that, "You can sell without serving but you can't serve without selling." While serving and sacrificing are important on a mere humanity level, they are also important in business. When you spend more time, energy, and focus on serving your customers than on serving yourself, you will sell more and gain more customers. Theodore Roosevelt said, "People don't care how much you know until they know how much you care." Unfortunately, with my thick skull and bad attitude it took this kind of stuff to get the concept through to me. Instead of "Serve others because you have more than them and it is important to care about people" it took something like "Serve others and you will make more sales" to make the difference. Oh wait, I will make more money if I put others first? Deal. I know I know, I am sick and twisted, but surely, I am not the only one.

When this hit me, I thought, okay I can do that. It felt as if there was a bigger purpose behind it than only something fluffy and nice. That purpose was my own selfish gain, but it was a start and if it needs to be your start too, that is okay. What I learned is that if you serve only for selfish gain it does not yield the same results. When I walked into a room with my focus on service because my underlying focus was on myself, well, I did not sell very much. However, when I worked on changing my heart to serve the people in the room without allowing personal gain to be my primary thought then everything changed. Realize what Andy Horner said is true, but your heart has to be with the people, not on the personal gain. When your intention is to serve people, in whatever capacity, you will inevitably gain something yourself. Whether it be sales specifically, or something else…only you can go out and discover what that is.

*****

There you have it. My hodgepodge collection of chapters sharing some of the most important things I believe our parents taught us growing up. Much of this I did not realize I was being taught at the time. My parents did not necessarily teach us the steps to determine our values or point out how sacrificially they lived their lives for the sake of others and their country. What they did was just live it out. They did not have to *tell* me to "be a strong female" they just raised me to *be* a strong female. Instead of telling us so many things, they simply lived their lives in a way they thought was right and hoped we would do the same. We watched them sacrifice, work hard, work together and boldly threaten the status quo at nearly every turn of their lives. And it made me who I am today. Because of them you are holding this book and reading these concepts. My greatest desire is that this book would challenge, maybe even irk you a little bit, to do something differently. Whether that is to courageously pursue something you have been putting off (like writing a book), doing the work to determine your values so that you can live your life intentionally by those values, to seek out new employment, new friends, new faith or to change the way you think. My challenge to you is to quit accepting "Normal" as your way of life. To have the courage to take life head on, do things that matter and commit to being a successful, useful and loving human being. Accept that quitting is not an option, everything worth anything will take hard work and be bold to stand up for what you believe in, *not* what is popular. Threaten the status quo every chance you get. OORAH!

Semper Fi.

"Excellence is never an accident. It is always the result of high intention, sincere effort, and intelligent execution; it represents the wise choice of many alternatives – choice, not chance, determines your destiny." - Aristotle

<u>Keep Growing:</u>
>   *Seven* by Jen Hatmaker
>   *Leaders Eat Last* by Simon Sinek
>   *Redeeming Love* by Francine Rivers
>   *Love Does* by Bob Goff
>   *The Meaning of Marriage* by Timothy Keller

What did you think of *Marine Corps B.R.A.T.?*
Thank you for purchasing this book!
I hope it added value and quality to your life.

If you enjoyed this book and found some benefit in reading
it, I would like to hear from you! Please send me your
feedback by leaving a review on Amazon.com.
Your feedback and support will help make me a better
author and greatly improve my writing for future projects.
Thank you!

Connect with Kylee N. Robinson on Instagram:
@kylee_n_robinson

Made in the USA
Middletown, DE
24 June 2021